D0910345

FOUL DEEDS AND SUSPICIOUS DEATHS AROUND THE TEES

Foul Deeds and Suspicious Deaths Around

THE TEES

Maureen Anderson

Series Editor
Brian Elliott

Wharncliffe Books

First Published in 2002 by
Wharncliffe Books
an imprint of
Pen and Sword Books Limited,
47 Church Street, Barnsley,
South Yorkshire. S70 2AS

Copyright © Maureen Anderson

For up-to-date information on other titles produced under the
Wharncliffe imprint, please telephone or write to:

> **Wharncliffe Books**
> **FREEPOST**
> **47 Church Street**
> **Barnsley**
> **South Yorkshire S70 2BR**
> **Telephone (24 hours): 01226 - 734555**

ISBN: 1-903425-26-3

All rights reserved. No part of this publication may be
reproduced, stored in a retrieval system, or transmitted, in
any form or by any means, electronic, mechanical,
photocopying, recording or otherwise, without the prior
permission in writing of the publishers.

This book is sold subject to the condition that it shall not,
by way of trade or otherwise, be lent, resold, hired out or
otherwise circulated without the publisher's prior consent in
any form of binding or cover other than that in which it is
published and without a similar condition including this
condition being imposed on the subsequent purchaser.

A CIP catalogue record of this book is available from the
British Library

Cover illustration: *The Strangled Woman c. 1870-72.* The Art Archive/Musee d'Obay Paris/Dagli Orti

Printed in the United Kingdom by
CPI UK

Contents

Introduction

A sad but true fact is that murder and other atrocities amongst the human race have taken place since the dawn of civilisation and will continue to do so until the end of time. Man's inhumanity to man is carried out in different ways and cruel acts are performed for many reasons including anger, hate, jealousy, power and greed. One of the common causes for robbery or violence amongst the poorer classes in the nineteenth century were the effects of alcohol, especially cheap gin, which was readily available.

Sometimes the perpetrator of a crime might have originally been the victim. They have tolerated mental or physical abuse until they can take no more and eventually retaliate against their tormentor.

Until the early twentieth century, ignorance, cramped conditions, poverty and a lack of hygiene causing disease, contributed to the infant mortality rate being extremely high. Single mothers would be outcasts or left with no choice but to take the worst and most menial positions available. Very often their babies were stillborn, or were they? If nobody attended to them at the birth it would have been relatively easy to suffocate, or do some other form of fatal injury to the child, and then claim the child was stillborn. Large families were common, but it was not so common for every baby to reach even the walking stage. The poorer households must have despaired when their families increased to more than could be afforded.

Although one would like to believe there would have been maternal and paternal love from many parents, perhaps there would have been a secret sigh of relief when an infant died of some natural cause, with the prominent thought being that now there was one less mouth to feed. Men and women of the poorer classes often worked long, hard hours earning just enough to keep starvation at bay. Perhaps in many cases of children murdered by parents, with no one to turn to for help, for an instant the pressures became too great and a form of insanity took over just long enough to carry out the dreadful deed. Whatever the reasons leading to a crime such as this, what is incomprehensible is the cruel manner in which the life of an innocent child was sometimes ended.

Some young men who could not get work in their area, or who perhaps thought that to go to sea was an adventure, would join a ship's crew and some were forced into the work by the press gangs. On board ship the captain was the law and all too many of them were hard, tough men who treated their crew, especially the younger members, with cruelty and savagery. If death took place at sea resulting from ill-treatment, the body could be thrown overboard, the rest of the crew often too frightened to speak up, so many crimes aboard ships would have never come to light. There were also cases of mutiny from crew members, either for gain or hatred of the captain.

Coroners have been used since the twelfth century, their job being to investigate sudden, violent or suspicious deaths and to decide what and who was the cause. Bodies were taken to the nearest public room for a medical examination and for the jury to view. The public room was often an inn, so no doubt these unpleasant tasks would be accompanied by a jar or two of ale! Very often the verdict on the body would simply be 'found dead.' If the 'accused' was found guilty, he or she would be committed to the nearest assizes for trial and sentencing, in our area it was usually either York or Durham.

Limited knowledge of forensic evidence meant that often the perpetrator of a crime would not be brought to justice, or even if they were they would not be convicted. Autopsies became more thorough towards the end of the nineteenth century as the knowledge of forensic evidence improved.

The manner in which some of these crimes have been carried out in these accounts is almost beyond belief, but they are all true. The cases have been found in chronologies of the area written by historians and by painstaking research in North-East newspapers. Sometimes, reading these publicised accounts, it appears that quite often a murder or serious crime would go unpunished because of class distinction. If the victim was a beggar or from a very poor family there often seemed to be little effort made to find the persons responsible unless it was blatantly obvious. In most cases the victim would know the perpetrator of the crime. A criminal who was of the upper class or, as in one of the cases related here, a member of the clergy and under the protection of the church, perhaps would have a less serious charge brought against them than the actual crime the evidence points to and, therefore, the punishment would not be so harsh as might have been deserved. Clergy were very rarely sentenced to death, as this would have been an embarrassment to the church.

Foul Deeds and Suspicious Deaths Around the Tees, published by Wharncliffe Books is part of a series that is proving extremely popular. The cases related in this book span 100 years, giving an insight into the poverty and ignorance of the poorer working classes that was all too often at the root of the depravity that led to a foul deed being committed.

I owe a debt of gratitude to Jim, my partner and friend, for all his support and patience. My sincere thanks also go to all the staff at Wharncliffe and to Series Editor, Brian Elliott for his invaluable advice throughout the writing of this book.

Chapter 1

The Punishment of Mary Nicholson
1799

From a house in Newtown, near to Little Stainton, the Ord family had just retired to bed at about nine o'clock. Mr Ord heard a knock at the door so he called out asking who it was. A female voice answered, begging to be admitted and pleading for a bed for the night, as she was lost and very cold. Mr Ord, being a kind man, let her in and after a few questions, said he would give her a bed but told her she must leave on the following morning. The young girl told him that she was the servant of Mr John Atkinson at Little Stainton. Had Mr Ord known what had transpired prior to this visit, he perhaps would not have been so welcoming.

The girl was an orphan named Mary Nicholson. She had been sexually abused and ill-used by her master for some time. She must have come to a point where she could stand it no longer, so decided to kill him. One morning she went to

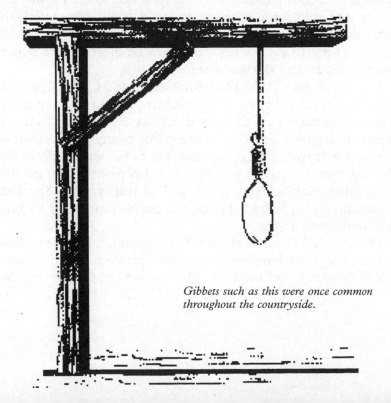

Gibbets such as this were once common throughout the countryside.

Darlington and purchased some arsenic from an apothecary, returned home and mixed it with some flour. Her master was away from home at the time but expected back that afternoon. His elderly mother, Elizabeth, made a pudding for him using the deadly mixture. On John's return, however, he told his mother he had already eaten and was not hungry. The frugal old lady mixed the pudding with some more of the flour, added a few other ingredients and made up a large family cake for the following morning's breakfast.

The family all had a portion of the cake, but, of course, Mary declined and within a very short space of time the Atkinsons were seriously ill. A doctor was sent for immediately and under his ministrations, all recovered except for Elizabeth. She lasted for a few weeks in great pain, and then died.

John Atkinson was in no doubt that this had been Mary's doing, perhaps his conscience told him why she had taken these measures, so he felt he had to be lenient. He told the girl to leave and he would not take the matter any further as long as she never darkened his door again and never returned to Little Stainton.

Mary had left and wandered about for days alone and destitute before knocking on the door of the Ord's house. On leaving the following morning, she returned to the Atkinson's house and told John Atkinson that she could not cope with what she had done, was in torment and could not rest, so he may send her to gaol or do with her as he pleased. The police were called in and she was arrested.

Her trial began at the Durham Assizes on 31 July 1798 and she was found guilty of wilful murder. The twelve presiding judges, because of some point of law that could not be decided, deferred sentence on Mary. For nearly twelve months Mary, not knowing what her fate was to be, was made to do domestic work in the prison and was also passed amongst the local inhabitants to work for them and run errands. She was eventually brought back before the twelve judges on 16 July and sentenced to death.

On 22 July 1799 a huge crowd of spectators, some who had travelled a very long distance, assembled on Framwellgate Moor to watch the hanging. Mary stood on the cart as the

A female about to be hanged in the eighteenth century.

noose was placed around her neck. The cart was pulled away and she stayed suspended from the rope for a minute or so, then to the gasps of the crowd, the rope broke and she fell to the ground. To the great distress of the onlookers, Mary lay on the ground gasping for breath, her eyes bulging and her body twitching. She slowly regained her faculties and conversed with those around her. It was almost an hour before another rope was procured, the execution was resumed and Mary Nicholson's torment was ended as she was launched into eternity.

Chapter 2

The Changed Will
1822

When Robert Peat found out his half-cousin, an elderly man, also by the name of Robert Peat, because he had offended him, had changed his will he decided something would have to be done. The original will, written in 1808, had left Robert a legacy but the new will, drawn up in 1815, left everything to his half-cousin's wife.

Robert lived at Ravensworth, near Richmond and every market day he visited Darlington and went to see his half-cousin and his wife. He was not a welcome visitor because of the altercation that had taken place between them, but still he insisted on these weekly excursions.

On 10 June he told a neighbour that he was going to wait until the old woman went to market, 'who he said wanted to wrong him out of the "brass" he had' and steal the wills. Later he told the neighbour that he had the wills in his possession. He also showed him a bottle of laudanum saying he wished the old woman had it and that 'it would do her a trick.'

On Monday 24 June Robert made his usual visit. The old lady had put a leg of lamb in some water to stew on the fire and had gone out to the market twice. When she returned to the house the second time Robert told her he had waited in the house during her absence and that his half-cousin had stayed in an adjoining room. He then went on to tell her that he had read in the papers that some people had been poisoned by bad water and asked her if she had heard about it. She replied that she had more to do than sit and read the papers. When Robert left a few minutes later the old man joined his wife and they ate some of the stew. (He would not sit in the same room as Robert) The couple ate the lamb,

A sketch of the 'hanging room' at Durham Gaol.

which they thought had a peculiar taste. Both of them became violently ill. Robert returned at 4 o'clock and saw them vomiting. He returned at about 6 o'clock and looked through the window. A neighbour, Mary Bolam, who was trying to assist the old couple, asked Robert to go for a doctor but he refused saying that he didn't want the old lady to know he was still in the town, yet he visited again at ten that night and wanted to stay. Mary Bolam told him he should go home, which he did. No doctor was called in and the old lady died that night.

Before eating the stew, she had given a little of it to some of her neighbours. They all became ill and later all said that the lamb had a strange flavour and was a 'very dark' colour.

The laudanum had been purchased from John Smith, a chemist in Darlington. Robert had told Smith that it was for some ladies at Middleton. When an investigation eventually started, Robert went back to Smith and asked if he remembered him, saying that he was getting the blame for murder but he still had the laudanum at home.

Amazingly, it was to be four weeks after the old lady was buried before Robert was charged with her murder. Before he was taken to prison, he wrote to his wife directing that she tell their son to give up the wills and he added 'Think no more of me, my chance is very bad.'

Robert was right about his chances being bad. He was hanged at Durham on 9 August 1822.

Chapter 3

Death on the High Seas
1855-92

In the middle of the nineteenth century, Hartlepool and West Hartlepool were busy and prosperous shipping ports, which meant that many of the residents of the town were merchants, ship owners and ships' underwriters. Cargoes of coal, loam and many other commodities were taken from the Hartlepool Docks to every part of the world. It would sometimes be months and even years before a vessel would return to its homeport. These tedious and confining months at sea, in close proximity to a small number of men, would cause tempers to rise, nerves to fray, and sometimes would be a recipe for disaster.

1855: Mutiny on Board

A merchant and ship owner of West Hartlepool received a telegraphic message on 6 July from his brig *Her Majesty*, at the time moored at Queenstown in Ireland. The message was to report a mutiny and the deaths of the captain, W Wright, (from Whitby) the mate, Samuel Cole and the cook, Thomas Vicks. Two other members of the crew had been wounded severely. The brig had sailed from Hartlepool with nine crew, one of

Hartlepool Docks in 1889. Pattison's Pictures, Bowes Museum

whom was an Irishman, James Veale, who it was said, had been violent and argumentative since the start of the voyage. The captain had written several entries in his logbook about the man's misconduct.

The captain did his usual round of the vessel at ten o'clock, and finding that Veale was not at his watch where he should be, set out to look for him. He found him in the galley-house, asleep. The captain went for a bucket of water and threw it over Veale and then walked to the port side of the deck. Veale awoke in a towering rage and went onto the deck. As he came face to face with the captain, he drew out a large case knife and without hesitation stabbed the man repeatedly. At the captain's cries, three of the watch came running to see him lying on the deck with Veale on top of him still stabbing his already badly mutilated body. One of the crew shouted to fetch the mate; on hearing this Veale stood up and headed for the mate's cabin. Two of the crewmen and an apprentice ran for the safety of the captain's cabin, shouting a warning to the mate as they did so. The mate had been asleep and was caught unawares. He was heard to cry out 'God! What's the matter?' Veale then stabbed him three times. Just after this, a cabin boy, from where he was hiding, heard two splashes. As the bodies of the captain and the mate were not found on board, Veale must have thrown them into the sea. Still with murderous intent, Veale then went to the forecastle where two of the crewmen lay asleep. He

Whitby Harbour, 1889. Pattison's Pictures, Bowes Museum

stabbed them both, the cook was killed and the other seaman, John Bull was badly injured. Meanwhile the crew who had made it to the captain's cabin, searched for firearms. George Bald found a pistol and came out of the cabin to look for Veale but the murderer came up from behind him and stabbed him in the back and neck. Bald fell and the pistol went off. Veale picked up the pistol and went back to the forecastle, then took up an axe and tried to scuttle the ship. Bald meanwhile, although injured, had found a loaded musket and sneaking to the forecastle managed to shoot Veale in the leg, which slowed him down, Bull fired again but thought the shot had not found its mark. Later it was found that the shot had penetrated the lungs and abdomen. Veale then lay down and went to sleep. John Bull managed to creep out from the forecastle to join his comrades who hoisted signals of distress. These were seen by the *Isabella*, which pulled alongside. The captain and mate from the *Isabella* called to Veale to give himself up, but by this time he must have been in great pain because he begged them to shoot him. They refused, saying they were going to bring him to justice and they then returned to their vessel to procure assistance. When they returned with back-up to the brig, Veale was dead. He had tried to hang himself with his belt and when this did not work he had used his knife to cut his own throat.

So ended the mutiny on *Her Majesty*.

1857: The Torture of Andrew Rose

The Sunderland-owned barque *Martha and Jane* sailed from West Hartlepool in 1856 heading for Calcutta, Demerara and Barbados where there was a change of master, and a considerable change of crew. The new captain was Henry Rogers, aged thirty-seven, a master mariner; his two mates were William Miles aged twenty-seven and Charles Seymour aged twenty-five. A young man, Andrew Rose, signed on at Barbados as an able seaman on 20 April 1857, knowing eventually the barque would return to Hartlepool.

Rose was not a very bright lad but he was a willing worker. Immediately after boarding the vessel he was given a task, but did not perform it to Seymour's satisfaction so he was badly beaten. Some of the crew advised him to run away while they

A brig and barque entering Hartlepool Harbour in the nineteenth century. Author's
Collection

were still in port. He did so, but on 10 May the police found
him and delivered him back to the vessel where he was put in
irons. On 11 May the *Martha and Jane* sailed from Barbados.
Less than a month later, Rose was dead.

A few days after leaving port, Rose was released from the
irons but was beaten continuously almost every day by Rogers
and the first and second mate. One Sunday, Rose was sitting
on the forecastle singing the hymn, *Oh Be Joyful*, when Rogers
told him to stop singing, then ordered Miles and Seymour to
bring an iron bolt. The bolt was forced into Rose's mouth, tied
on around his head and he was left wearing this item of torture
for well over an hour, which must have caused him extreme
pain and discomfort.

Rose was made to sleep on deck instead of the forecastle
with the other men. On one occasion he climbed into one of
the small boats and pulled some sailcloth over himself to keep
warm but was made to get back on the deck and sleep with no
covering. He was given only bread and water to eat and the
crew was told if they fed him any meat they would get the same
treatment. On one occasion he was left without any food at all
for twenty-four hours.

Rogers had a dog called Watch, which he instructed to 'bite
that man.' The dog, every time Rose was beaten, would fly at

him and bite pieces out of his legs and if Rose put his hands down to protect himself, Watch would bite his arms.

On one occasion, Rose was ordered to climb up the mast and furl the sails, on his return to deck, he was forced to strip naked, given a bucket of water and made to climb back up. Seymour climbed up behind, whipping Rose all the way. On two occasions, when he was in irons, he was not released to perform the toilet and he soiled the deck. Both times Rogers took a small shovel and fed the youth his own excrement, at the same time filling his nose with it until he could not breath and had to swallow. After this, because his trousers were soiled, they were thrown overboard and he was left

A set of manacles or irons of the type used to restrain Andrew Rose. The Author

For twelve hours Andrew Rose was confined in a ship's water barrel such as these. The bung hole would have been the only source of fresh air. The Author

naked. The terrible torture continued with Rose being put into a water cask, which was then sealed, with only the tiny space in the bung hole for air, and rolled up and down the deck. He was then left in the cask from twelve noon until twelve at night.

The final cruelty came one day with Rogers saying to the youth 'I wish you would drown or hang yourself,' to which Rose replied that the master may as well do it. Rogers then made a timber hitch or 'running noose' and putting it around Rose's neck, hoisted him onto the yardarm, keeping him there for two or three minutes. When he was dropped, his skin was turning black, his tongue hanging out, his eyes staring from their sockets and he could not stand. He was taken to the forecastle, but by this time his mind had gone and he was gradually sinking.

On 5 June, some of the crew pulled him with a rope onto the deck. They were loath to touch him because of the dreadful state he was in. He had wounds all over his body, which had festered and the bites he had received from the dog were infected with maggots. The following day he died, and Rogers ordered his body thrown overboard without a prayer or any ceremony.

There had been fourteen men on the barque. The crew members that were not involved in the atrocities reported the murder as soon as they reached the next port, which was Liverpool. All ten testified as witnesses at the ensuing trial. They stated that they could not have intervened because they would have then received the same treatment. They all agreed that while Rose was not very bright, he never disobeyed an order and none of them knew why the three men had inflicted the barbaric cruelties upon him.

At the trial held at the Lancashire Assizes in Liverpool, the solicitor for the three prisoners stated that Roger's records showed that he had been at sea for many years, first as a seaman then as a mate before becoming the captain of a vessel. There had never been complaints about him. Also in the prisoner's defence, he said that Rose was stubborn, inattentive to his duties, had filthy habits and had provoked the captain almost beyond measure.

The prosecution showed that this character assassination was not true. Rose was originally from Gosport on the Isle of

Wight. He had been living in Hartlepool for many years. His wife was Ann Pyeman, who was the daughter of an innkeeper in the town. Rose had sailed in many vessels from Sunderland and Hartlepool and left them all with a good character for conduct and hard work. It was also stated that if there was mutiny or misconduct aboard ship, the person should be placed in irons and conveyed to the proper authorities. It was not for the captain or crew to take that person's life, especially by the means in which Rose's life was taken.

All three men were found guilty of wilful murder and sentenced to death. Mr Snowball, town clerk of Sunderland, the prisoners' solicitor and others campaigned for the men's release. Mr Snowball travelled to London to meet with the Home Secretary to plead their case. Three days before the executions were to take place, the Home Secretary, George Grey, sent word that the sentences of Miles and Seymour were to be changed to penal servitude for life but the sentence of death was to remain on Rogers.

On Saturday 11 September, the scaffold was erected at the north-west corner of Kirkdale Gaol in Liverpool. From there, ironically, was an extensive view of the docks and the channel filled with sailing vessels. This, and the huge crowd of spectators that had assembled, would be the last thing that Henry Rogers would ever see. The terrible cruelty and death that was inflicted on Andrew Rose, at least as far as legal justice was concerned, was avenged.

1859: The Murder of Captain Barker

The barque *Margaret* sailed from West Hartlepool with a cargo of coke on 12 July with a crew of thirteen and the master, Phillip Barker, who was from Stockton. Barker was said to be a kind man but particular about the management of his vessel. Arriving in Lisbon on 28 July, the cook and steward became ill and were taken to hospital. The captain employed a twenty-three-year-old Portuguese seaman, Charles Annois, to take over the tasks of the absent crew members. The *Margaret* sailed from Lisbon on 11 August and all was well until 18 August when an altercation took place between Annois and some of the other members of the crew. The captain heard the

A barque leaving Hartlepool Harbour in the nineteenth century. Pattison's Pictures, Bowes Museum

commotion and on asking what was the matter, was told that Annois was refusing to wash the dinner things and had called the men bad names. The captain told the crew that he would not have any man aboard his ship imposed upon and neither would he have name-calling. This was perhaps because Annois was the only man aboard that was not British and he may have felt that because of this the men were being prejudicial towards him. He then told Annois that he was to wash up after the meal every evening because that was part of his job.

Things remained quiet on board until a few nights later. Richard Faux, the second mate, was on watch until midnight when Thomas Sharpe, the first mate, relieved him. Faux then went to the captain's cabin, which was on the starboard side of the vessel, and reported the state of the weather to him before going to his own cabin where Annois was asleep. Faux was woken at four in the morning to stand watch again and when he arrived on deck he saw Annois in the act of getting dressed and a little later going into the cook's galley. Sharpe and the rest of the crew had all gone to bed by this time. Annois then came out of the galley and went to the captain's cabin. A few minutes later, Faux heard a scream and saw Annois standing on deck near the longboat with a knife held between his teeth and a five barreled revolver that had belonged to the captain in his hand. Faux went to the captain's cabin and found him lying in a pool of blood, his throat had been cut so deeply that his head was nearly severed from his body. Faux shouted an alarm and then went to alert the first mate but his cabin had been locked from the outside. Between the two of them they managed to break the door open, as they did so they saw Annois approaching, so went to find weapons with which to defend themselves. They armed themselves with a saw and a screwdriver and went back up on deck. By this time Annois had attacked and slashed the face of Joe Cummings, one of the crewmembers with whom he had argued at the beginning of the voyage. The first mate shouted to the crew to find weapons of some sort and told them that the revolver that was in Annois' possession belonged to the captain and was never kept loaded. Annois had by this time, shut himself in the captain's cabin and was smashing everything in it. The first mate and some of the crew went to the skylight, broke some of the panes of glass and threw them down on Annois. He came out of the cabin, threw his arms up and shouted 'Me kill captain, me kill no more people.' The crew rushed at him and secured him, besides the large galley knife he also had a table knife hidden in a wide sash that was tied around his arm, it was this he had used to cut Joe Cummings face.

When questioned about what he had done, he said it was because the captain had given him too much work and that he been going to kill five more men.

The Margaret was brought to anchor at Falmouth and Annois was arrested. He told the police his real name was Francisco Antonio. For his trial he was offered the option of a jury composed of one half foreign and one half English or all Englishmen, he elected to be tried by a jury of Englishmen. He pleaded not guilty and a Mr Metcalfe of the Portuguese Consul was elected to defend him. Annois denied having any recollection of the deeds he had carried out. He also said that he had nothing against the captain and had meant him no harm. When all the evidence had been heard the jury was instructed that the prisoner was certainly guilty of murder but they must decide whether he had committed the act in a moment of insanity, in which case he would be locked away where he could do no more harm, or whether he was of sound mind and should be sent to the scaffold. The jury found him to be of sound mind and guilty of wilful murder. The judge donned his black cap and told the prisoner that it was not his duty to dwell on the enormity of the deed that had been committed, merely pass upon him the sentence that the law directed for the dreadful crime for which he had been found guilty.

The Portuguese consul took up the case and made a strong representation to the Home Secretary for a reprieve, believing Annois had committed the act in a moment of insanity. They asked for a stay of execution until evidence pertaining to his mental health could be obtained from his home at Rio de Janeiro. The Home Secretary granted a reprieve for a fortnight. Because the information had still not arrived, two further fortnight's reprieves were given.

The date for the execution was finally set for 26 April 1860. There is no record of Annois being hanged so maybe he was saved from the scaffold and detained in an asylum instead.

1866: A Rather Suspicious Tale

The *Ann and Sarah* in the charge of Captain Taylor returned in February to West Hartlepool after a five month long voyage to the Baltic. Immediately after the vessel had docked, Captain Taylor went to see Sergeant Davidson of the West Hartlepool Constabulary. He related to him a strange and suspicious account of the events that had supposedly taken place while the *Ann and Sarah* was at sea.

In December, one of the crew-members, Benjamin Mole, had taken ill and was left behind. An Irishman, Michael Wire, took his place. Besides the crew there was also a disabled passenger, William Day, on board who had joined the ship at Welborg in November. On the evening of Christmas Day, Captain Taylor had gone ashore to purchase some provisions in the ship's boat, which was manned by Henry Bower, Michael Wire, Charles Miller (who was Swedish) and William Day. The Captain told the men to take the provisions the value of which was £15, back to the *Ann and Sarah*, which was at anchor a short distance out to sea, then return to shore and collect him in the afternoon. They did not come back and although Captain Taylor telegraphed along the coast to try to find them, it was to no avail.

On 27 December the boat was found in Sweden on the opposite coast to where it should have been. William Day was lying dead in the bottom of the boat with his head in a few inches of freezing seawater. The other three men were drunk, having helped themselves to a keg of gin that was amongst the provisions. Bowyer had some scratches on his face, Wire had two black eyes and the dead man also had a black eye. The body was removed to the hospital at Ellsinore and the three men were taken before the Vice Consul. Because of the suspicious circumstances they were detained in custody until the *Ann and Sarah* picked them up.

Their story was that when the captain had sent them off with the provisions, a thick fog had come down, and they could not find the vessel nor return to the Danish shore, two days later their boat landed on the Swedish coast. Bowyer said he received the scratches when he fell on some rocks and Wire said his black eyes were from falling against the side of the boat. All three insisted that William Day had died from the cold.

The three men were brought before two justices of the peace to be questioned and they related the same story that had been told to Captain Taylor.

The two learned gentlemen came to the conclusion that as there were no witnesses except the three seamen themselves and their story sounded plausible they could only dismiss the case. They did however, admonish Captain Taylor for sending the men off on their own with a keg of gin.

1884: Tragedy or Murder

Two firemen joined the *Reindeer* as she sailed from Middlesbrough to Cronstadt on Sunday 15 June. One was Thomas Finclain and the other George Scott. The chief engineer on board was George Kitson of Brunswick Street, West Hartlepool.

On the morning of 18 June, Finclain and Scott went to the stoke-hole to relieve the two firemen who were on duty. Shortly afterwards Kitson appeared and asked Scott if he had cleared one of the furnaces in the stoke-hole. Scott replied that he had and Kitson then told him to clear the ashes that had come out of the fire. Scott went over to Kitson and made a rude remark. Kitson punched Scott in the face and knocked him down. Scott stood up and shouted out, which brought the captain, James Gallert, running. Instead of quieting the situation though, he punched Scott, knocking him against the bunker. Kitson pulled the captain off Scott saying he would do it himself. The captain then left the stoke-hole and Scott began to shift the ashes. The two firemen worked on until breakfast, after they had eaten they both returned to work. About half an hour later Kitson came back and stood over Scott while he cleaned up some more ashes. Scott then went on deck for some water. He was away about fifteen minutes so Kitson said he was going to look for him. Kitson returned and said to Finclain that Scott was on deck sitting on a hatch. When Scott eventually returned, Kitson told Finclain to make himself scarce for an hour. After half an hour or so, Finclain heard Scott shouting for him and that he was being murdered. A short time later Finclain saw Scott trying to climb up the ladder to the deck, his face bleeding. Scott made the attempt several times but Kitson kept pulling him back down. Eventually Kitson left him alone but by then Scott was too weak to climb the ladder and he passed out in the stoke-hole. By this time it was noon. At four o'clock Finclain procured assistance to carry Scott onto the deck. When they got him there he was dead. Scott's face was bruised and swollen, his shirt and trousers badly torn and covered in blood.

Another fireman, Alexander Cutfield, had also seen Scott struggling to climb the ladder. At one point Kitson could not pull Scott back down by his legs, so he had climbed above and kicked him down. Three of the other crew had also heard Scott shouting and seen him trying to climb up on deck. One shouted to Kitson to ask what was wrong and Kitson replied nothing was the matter it was just Scott's laziness.

When the *Reindeer* reached London there was an inquest into Scott's death. The crew told their stories and all said that George Scott had been in good health when the vessel set sail from Middlesbrough.

The inquest decided that Kitson had hit Scott under extreme provocation and that the chief engineer had a perfect right to insist on discipline. It was said that George Scott was suffering from the great heat and probably seasickness. No excessive violence had been used so he had therefore died from natural causes and Kitson was exonerated of any blame.

1892: The Cargo

A short article that was published in an unknown newspaper in 1892 is worth a mention because of the name of the vessel concerned in the event. It was the steamship *Durham*. Carrying a cargo of ballast, the vessel sailed from Millbank Wharf in London to Cardiff. On arrival at the dock a gang of men were employed to unload the cargo. They had not been working long when a terrible odour began to emanate from the ballast. They continued working for a little longer when suddenly the source of the smell became obvious as they were confronted with human skulls, bones and rotting wood. All the men went to the captain and told him they would only finish unloading the cargo if they received extra pay. Their demand was granted and work was resumed. The stench became so vile the men were obliged to resort to 'stimulants' to prevent them being sick (a tot or two of rum no doubt).

It was later ascertained that the ballast had come from Millbank Prison, which was being demolished at the time, (now the site of the Tate Gallery) and the bones were those of criminals that were executed there. At one time the bodies of executed criminals were dissected but the practice was abolished in 1832.

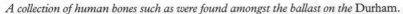

A collection of human bones such as were found amongst the ballast on the Durham.

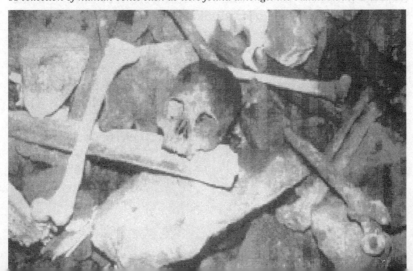

Chapter 4

The Middlesbrough Mystery
1855

Ann Kitchen was a good natured, happy, seventeen-year-old girl who lived in and worked as a servant for a provision dealer, Christopher Wright, and his wife. They had employed her at the Mayday hirings fair. One Tuesday evening in August at about 9 o'clock, she had been sent for a message from Mr Penny's chemist shop and had returned to the house a few minutes later. A little after nine her employers noticed she was missing and became concerned, as she had never disappeared without telling them where she was going. They waited until 10 o'clock and when she still had not returned, Mr Wright went out to look for her. Not finding any sign of Ann he went home just after midnight and left the latch off the door in case she returned while they were in bed.

The following day Ann had still not appeared and Mrs Wright spoke to Mary Ann Jones who lived next door. Mary said she had spoken to Ann at about two thirty on Tuesday afternoon. Ann had been hanging out washing and she had told Mary that she was not to say anything until the next morning but this would be the last time she would wash for the Mrs or herself 'forever more' and that she had told her mistress she was leaving and her mistress had cried. Mary asked why she was going, was it because she was unhappy? Ann replied to the effect that the master and mistress were very kind, but she was unhappy and had been thinking of leaving for a month or more, but would still not say why she was leaving. Later, at about 7 o'clock, Ann spoke to Mary again saying that she had some unfinished chores but she would complete them 'so her employers would have nothing to say,' she was then going to the chemist on a message and afterwards she was leaving. They spoke again just after nine the same evening when Ann said goodbye because she would never return. Mary asked if she was leaving Middlesbrough and Ann answered 'a little bit but not far'; she then repaid Mary 6d (2.5p) she owed her. Mary asked if she was going to kill herself and Ann had said there was no danger of her doing that, and insisted again that Mary say nothing until the following morning. Mary also told Mrs Wright that she had often seen Ann in the company of a quack doctor and had seen her talking to men in the archway beside the houses. On Monday night she had seen her talking to two men, one of whom was wearing a white jacket, she had heard Ann telling him to go away in case her master came out of the house and saw them, the man had replied 'I don't give a damn for your master.' Mrs Wright said that Ann had not told her she was leaving but she recalled Ann telling her that a quack doctor, Mr Collinson, had asked her to be his sweetheart and to visit his surgery. Mrs Wright had told Ann if he bothered her again to let her know.

John Harris, a plasterer, on his way to catch a train to his work in Hartlepool at 5 o'clock on Wednesday morning, made a grim discovery. Near the ferry landing, lying with her feet and legs in the water and her head on the rough path, was the body of a young woman. It was Ann Kitchen.

Middlesbrough shipyard in the nineteenth century.. Pattison's Pictures, Bowes Museum

Ann had been seen just before 10 o'clock on Tuesday night between the shipyard and Durham Street heading towards the ferry landing by Martha Crowe who lived near the shipyard. Martha had called out to her as she passed but Ann just shook her head and hurried on. About twenty minutes prior to seeing Ann, Martha had noticed a young man in a white jacket standing at the bottom of the shipyard as if waiting for someone, but by the time Ann arrived he had gone.

The post-mortem on Ann revealed that she had recently engaged in sexual activity but the surgeon could not ascertain whether it was immediately prior to her death. It was also revealed that she was in the early stages of pregnancy. The cause of death was attributed to strangulation by drowning. There were no marks of violence on the body except for a cut on one eyelid that was thought might have been caused by a sharp object on the rough path her head was lying upon.

At the inquest, although a few witnesses were called the coroner dismissed their evidence as hearsay and accordingly it was not recorded, no light was shed upon the case so the jury's verdict was:

That the deceased was found drowned and suffocated without any external marks of violence on her person, but how or by what means she was drowned did not appear to the jurors.

Chapter 5

Watery Graves
1855-90

The winding River Tees and the mighty North Sea although providing a living and a means of transport and conveyance for many, also claimed lives. Accidental drowning was common, especially during the winter months when the river would swell and water would spill over its banks and storms would lash the coast so that the sailing vessels and their crews were at the mercy of the waves. On the more sinister side, the sea and the river also provided convenient graveyards in which to dispose of a body. The ebb and flow of the tide could more or less guarantee that if a body were washed up at all, it would be far from where it was originally put into the water.

The North Sea at Hartlepool during a storm. Pattison's Pictures, Bowes Museum

The King's Head Inn, *built in 1803, where the infant's body was taken for the inquest. Now the Seaton Hall nursing home.* Author's Collection

1855: Carr Sands

Robert Fawcett, a carpenter from West Hartlepool, was walking along the sands near Carr House at Seaton Carew one Sunday morning, when he saw a curiously shaped parcel floating at the water's edge. On pulling it onto the shore, he could see that the covering was a dark coloured petticoat pinned together round coarse cotton sheeting. On unwrapping the bundle Robert discovered the body of an infant. Leaving the body on a bank out of reach of the water he went to the nearest farmhouse to ask for assistance, he was advised to go to the village and alert PC Barton, the village constable.

The infant's body was taken to the *King's Head Inn*, which was situated beside the village green and run by Mrs Walker. Mr Longbotham, a surgeon from Greatham, examined the body and his findings were, that when the umbilical cord had been cut, it had not been tied and the infant had bled to death, which would have taken ten minutes or so. The surgeon felt that if this had not been the case the child had been healthy when born and would have survived.

At the inquest that followed this examination the jury came to the conclusion that the infant had been murdered, but they did not know by whom.

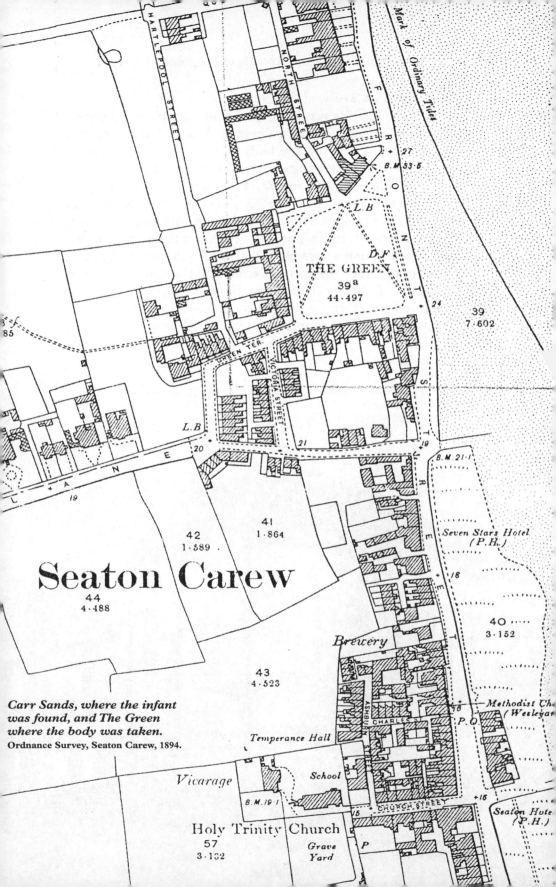

THE GREEN
39a
44·497

39
7·602

42
1·589

41
1·864

Seaton Carew

44
4·488

40
3·152

Brewery

Seven Stars Hotel (P.H.)

Methodist Ch (Wesleyan)

43
4·523

*Carr Sands, where the infant
was found, and The Green
where the body was taken.*
Ordnance Survey, Seaton Carew, 1894.

Temperance Hall

Vicarage

School

Holy Trinity Church
57
3·132

*Grave
Yard*

Seaton Hote (P.H.)

1867: Seaton Carew

As the morning tide was ebbing, William Crawford, an engine fitter from the village, was walking on Seaton Beach near the Sand Hole when he saw the body of a man lying on the sand just below the high water mark. The man's face was badly bruised but he did not appear to have been dead very long.

The body was taken to the *Seaton Hotel* where an inquest was held the next day. The man was in his mid-twenties, stout and well dressed, in his pockets were a watch chain with two keys attached, half a sovereign (50p), half a crown (12.5p) and some copper. His legs had old scorch marks upon them so it was deduced that he had probably been employed at some time in an iron furnace. People were called in from the local iron works to try to identify the body but no one knew him. A verdict of 'found dead' was reached and the body was interred with no further ado.

The Seaton Hotel, *1902, built as the* New Inn *in 1795. Inquests were often held here.* Author's Collection

The Royal Hotel *in the nineteenth century, where the inquest on the body of* *Robinson Lythe was held.* Author's Collection

1873: Swainson Dock

Mr R M Gallon's *Royal Hotel* in West Hartlepool was the venue for an inquest on the body of a young man, Robinson Lythe, who had been found floating in the water at Swainson Dock.

Lythe was only sixteen and worked at Messrs Rickinsons' wine and spirit stores in West Hartlepool. He was known to be a happy young man who enjoyed his job and did not get into any trouble. Lythe usually finished work at nine in the evening and always went straight home by a route that did not take him anywhere near the docks. On Friday 10 October at about six thirty, after he had bottled some wine, Lythe told a work colleague that if the master was looking for him he was just going across the yard and would not be long. The yard was at the back of Church Street about forty yards distance from the store. Lythe was not seen alive again.

To get to Swainson Dock, where his body was found the following day, he would have had to have crossed Church

Swainson Dock, where Robinson Lythe's body was found, and the Royal Hotel *in Church Street, West Hartlepool.* Ordnance Survey, West Hartlepool, 1896

Street and walked about 200 yards. There were no marks of violence on his body and no witnesses came forward to explain what had happened so a verdict of 'found dead' was recorded.

1878: The Slake

On 10 June, the body of a child was found floating in the water between the old harbour and The Slake at Hartlepool within the area enclosed by the lock gates. The gates were only occasionally opened to let the fishermen's boats in and out. Previous to the finding of the body, the gates had been opened on 4 June.

The body was of a female child and was wrapped in a dark brown, striped material, thought to perhaps have come from a lady's undergarment.

The Slake, Hartlepool, where the body of an infant was found. Extract from W O Mossman's map, 1851

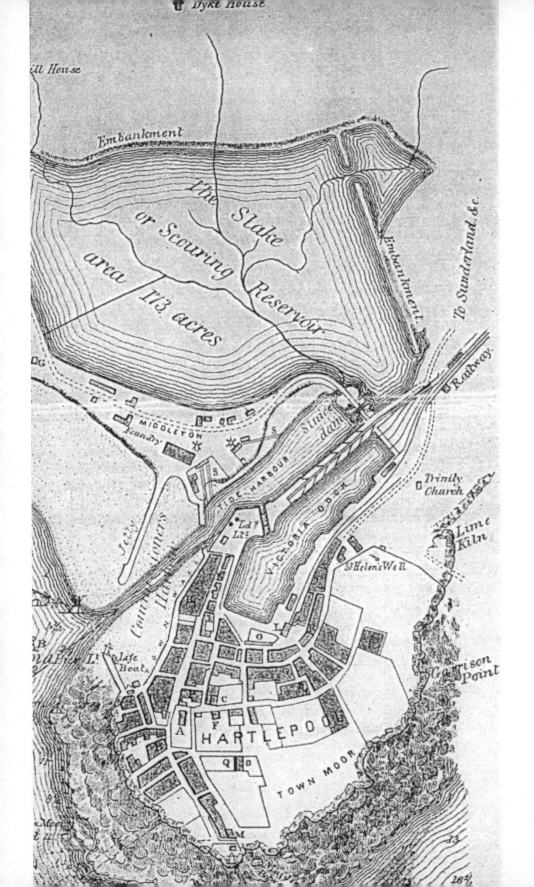

John Crow, physician, who examined the body found that there were two toes missing, two wounds and a bruise to the scalp. He thought the bruise had been caused during birth and the other injuries had taken place in the water after death. The child was newly born and had probably been in the water about four days. She had been born healthy and if cared for would have survived. The cause of death was the cord not being tied at birth and subsequently the child had bled to death. It was therefore murder. Although investigations were carried out, the mother was never apprehended.

1883: The South Pier

A storekeeper and a mast maker at Messrs Irvine and Co's harbour dockyard noticed something floating in the water. On closer inspection they found it to be the body of a man. They procured a boat hook and between them they dragged the body onto land. The man was quite stout and was dressed in a brown jacket and trousers, white moleskin waistcoat and a white overjacket. On his scalp was a slight wound that was still bleeding and there was an inch long gash to his throat.

The police were called and the body was removed to the dead house. Inspector Hutchinson made a search of the docks near to where the body was found. Behind an old marine boiler at the back of the yard, he found a fresh pool of blood, there were heel marks around the area but nothing to show that a struggle had taken place.

In his pockets the man had two sticks such as were used for measuring pit props, and a pocketknife, which had traces of blood and hair upon it. Neither of the wounds were deep enough to have been life threatening, the cause of death was by drowning.

A few days later, the body was identified as that of fifty-year-old George Lee, who had worked among the pit props on the dock. Prior to that employment he had worked as a cab driver for Mr Brown of the *Ward Jackson Hotel*. George had lodged at 12 Cromwell Street and was well thought of, as he had been involved with several Friendly Societies. His murder remained unsolved.

1890: The North Pier

Michael Coulson and his son were out sailing in their coble and as they neared the North Pier they saw the body of a man in the water near a bank of stones. The feet were tied and the length of cord had then been brought up behind the man's back to tie his hands. The eyes were no longer there, which was put down to him having been immersed in the water. They managed to pull the body into their coble and take it to shore, it was then conveyed to the dead house in Mainsforth Terrace.

The body was identified as a Dane, Lauritz Martineus Lassen, who was twenty. On his person were a five-shilling piece (25p), a silver shilling (5p), 6d (2.5p) in bronze, a

South and North Piers, West Hartlepool, where two bodies were found. Ordnance Survey, West Hartlepool, 1896

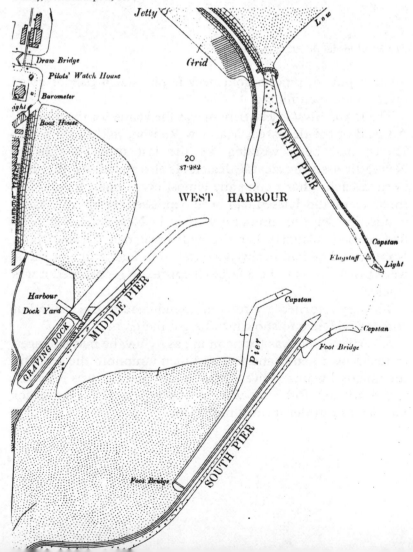

The Royal Hotel *in 2002.* The Author

tobacco pouch, pipe, a gold necktie pin and a pair of gold-faced solitaire cufflinks.

The *Royal Hotel* in Hartlepool was the venue for the inquest. A friend of the deceased, Matthew Robson, told the jury that Lassen had been working for the last three months in Newcastle assisting a cattle dealer. He also stated that they had been in each other's company almost every night for the last three weeks and Lassen had been depressed because he had a connection with an immoral woman in Newcastle. When he had refused to marry her she had threatened to shoot him. Robson said he had received a letter from Lassen the previous week that he took to be a farewell epistle, so he believed it was suicide.

The jury returned a verdict of 'found dead in the water, but without evidence to show how he got there.'

No explanation was forthcoming as to how he had managed to tie his own hands and feet and then jump into the sea. Did the immoral woman have a hand in his death or was it his so-called friend? Robbery was obviously not the motive for murder, as murder it must have been.

Chapter 6

Suffer the Little Children
1857-85

1857: John Stephen Cooke

In the village of Coxhoe, which lies south of Durham, resided a quarryman, his wife, Mary Cooke, and their two children William (aged eleven), and John Stephen (aged four). They all occupied one room on the lower floor of a two-roomed house, the upper floor, or loft was not used for domestic purposes.

It was considered in the village that Mary was not very bright. She came from a family where intelligence was lacking somewhat. Her brother had been nicknamed 'Fond Bobby' because he was thought feeble-minded. Mary was also profoundly deaf.

One Monday night in May, the father had gone out and the two boys, who slept in one bed, had retired at about 9 o'clock. Two hours later, the eldest boy William, awoke to feel his brother struggling beside him. By the light of the fire he could see blood on John's throat. As he sat up, he saw his mother coming towards him, also bleeding from the throat. He jumped out of bed, pulled on his trousers and ran to fetch his aunt, who lived next door. When he returned with his aunt, Mary was lying across the bed kicking and flailing her arms. The aunt could not restrain her, so ran to fetch her brother, Jeremiah Cooke, and to send for a surgeon. When they arrived at the house, William and his mother were standing by the fire. Mary was trying to staunch the blood coming from a wound in her throat. When she saw the surgeon and her brother enter the house, Mary threw herself on the bed again. Mr Carnes, the surgeon, managed to remove her and on doing so discovered the body of the youngest child, John. He had multiple slashes to his throat and his neck was nearly cut through with the ferocity of the attack. Mary had six cuts to

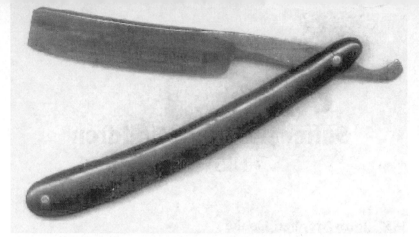

A razor similar to the one that was used by Mary Cooke. The Author

her own neck, one of which had severed her windpipe. Mr Carnes stitched the wounds and she was then able to speak, by this time PC Westall had arrived to take her into custody. Mary told her audience that sorrow and trouble had made her cut her child's throat with a razor that she had then thrown into the fire. She then took another razor to use on herself. At this point she became agitated again and tried to reopen her wounds, she was restrained with handcuffs.

A razor was later found in the ashes of the fire and another, heavily bloodstained, was found in a drawer.

It was rumoured in the village that jealousy of her husband had caused her to snap; if he stayed out late she thought he was with other women, although there were no foundations for suspicion. Because of her deafness, when she saw neighbours talking, she thought she was the subject of their conversation and that caused her to be suspicious.

The assumption at the initial trial was, that had the elder brother, William not awoken, he too would have been murdered and his mother would have succeeded in taking her own life. The jury returned a verdict of wilful murder and Mary was committed to trial at the Durham Assizes. But she died of her wounds before the trial took place. The charitable verdict given at the inquest on Mary's death was 'that she destroyed herself whilst labouring under temporary insanity,' thus giving a reason for the dreadful crime she had committed.

1857: A Gruesome Discovery at Freeborough Hill

While working on his farm one April day, Joseph Green was horrified when his dog brought him the gruesome remains of a child's leg. PC Dunn and Joseph began searching the area, and a few days later, about a mile away from where the leg was found, at the back of Freeborough Hill, the dog led the searchers to a child's shirt, a thighbone and head. The following day, at another spot, in a peat hole, there was found a few more items of clothing. It was ascertained on examination of the remains that there were eight wounds to the head and it had been severed from the body, all done with a sharp instrument.

Suspicions were eventually directed to Sarah Jamieson, who was about thirty-years-old and living as a housekeeper at Egton for a farm labourer, William Pearson, who was a widower with four children. It was known that Sarah had a child but Mr Pearson would not take it in as he had enough children of his own.

Sarah's baby boy was born in 1854, and her sister, Mrs Mead, had taken the child, who had been named Joseph, to be nursed by a Mrs Marley who lived in the town of Sleights. Sarah was to pay Mrs Marley to look after the child. On the night of 29 November of 1856, Sarah arrived at Mrs Marley's house to tell her she could not pay the £6. 8s (£6.40p) that she owed for Joseph but would pay as soon as she could. She said she was taking him away, perhaps to put in the poor house. Mrs Marley told her not to take Joseph at night but to come back the next day. When Sarah returned the following day to take him, he had on a plain white shirt that was slit on one sleeve because he had a sore arm. The shirt matched the one

Freeborough Hill, where Sarah Jamieson murdered her child. The Author

Roseberry Topping, another hill in the vicinity of Guisborough. The Author

that had been found by the dog.

Young William Pearson, the son of Sarah's employer, recalled her bringing the child to the house and asking if he would take them to Moorsholm. Sarah walked and young William carried the child on a donkey. When they were near to Freeborough Hill, Sarah told him to go and visit his relatives who lived nearby and she would meet him there later as she was going to take Joseph to Mangra Park, to leave him with some friends of hers, the Wilsons. Sarah arrived about two hours later to collect William and they then returned home.

A few months later Mrs Marley went to William Pearson's house to see Sarah about the money owed but did not get it. The following week Sarah turned up at Mrs Marley's house and told her that the little boy was staying with his father's sister beside Guisborough and that he was all right, adding as a joke that his uncle would kill him because he was fond of pulling the cows' tails. Mrs Marley asked if she had clothes for the child and she replied that the uncle had a boy of four years old that had died and Joseph was wearing his clothes.

When the police started making inquiries, Sarah left Mr Pearson's house without telling him she was going. The police apprehended her at Greenhow, when questioned as to the whereabouts of her child she gave a fictitious name and address as to where Joseph was. Eventually she broke down and told the police she had left him on the moors because she was destitute and could not afford to keep him but insisted that she had not hurt him.

At Guisborough petty sessions she was committed to the York Assizes for the wilful murder of her son.

Guisborough Town Hall in 2002; built in 1821, the petty sessions were held in the upper storey every Tuesday. The Author

At the trial the medical examiner testified that the wounds on the child's skull had been inflicted while he was still alive. The conclusion was that Sarah, while William was waiting for her at his relative's house, had murdered Joseph and then distributed his remains in as many places as she could, hoping he would never be found.

The jury found Sarah guilty of murder with a recommendation for mercy. The judge pronounced the death sentence and told her to prepare herself for eternity because he held out no hope for mercy. The plea for mercy was, however, heeded and her sentence was changed to life imprisonment.

1867: Michael O'Brien

Catherine O'Brien had a daughter, Mary Ann who was aged about thirteen, and a month old son, Michael. They lived in Cannon Street, Middlesbrough along with their cousins Thomas and Ellen Conaugh and an aunt. About two weeks before Michael was born, Catherine's husband, Andrew, had gone to America deserting his family and taking with him all the money they had.

Houses around Cannon Street, Middlesbrough in the nineteenth century. Cleveland County Council, Libraries and Leisure Department

One Sunday morning at about 6.30 am, Mary Ann was beside her mother's bed holding the baby in her arms when she told Thomas that the baby was dying. At this Catherine took the baby into her bed beside her where a few minutes later, he coughed as if choking and then died. For some inexplicable reason, a surgeon was not called until Sunday afternoon.

At the subsequent inquest held at the *Volunteer Hotel*, Cannonfield, Middlesbrough, it was revealed that the post mortem showed that Michael had died from suffocation. Mary Ann, Michael's sister was called to give evidence. Her story was, that early on Sunday morning Michael had been in bed with her mother and because she had no milk to give him, he was crying. Mary Ann had taken the baby and walked around the room with him and kissed him on the mouth, which she was in the habit of doing. Mary Ann then stated that her cousin Ellen was present when Michael died and although on the prior Saturday evening her aunt and her mother had shared a pint of ale, she had never seen her mother drunk.

Catherine's evidence was that when Mary Ann had handed the child back to her that Sunday morning, she had asked if she had been drawing his breath again and that in the past she had slapped her for kissing him on the lips and told her not to do it as it might harm the child. She said she tried to revive the baby by rubbing him and breathing into his mouth but he did not wake up.

Ellen Conaugh, gave contrary evidence by saying that she was not present when Michael died and knew nothing about the events until Sunday afternoon. Thomas stated that Mary Ann seemed to be trying to please the baby and it was not until he was handed to the mother that there was a problem.

The surgeon could not say how the suffocation was caused, he did not think it was by kissing the baby's lips but it could be that the mother 'overlaid' him.

The coroner and the jury did not believe either mother or daughter as to what had happened but decided to give them the benefit of the doubt, as there was no real evidence as to how Michael had met his death. The coroner admonished Catherine, telling her she'd had a narrow escape and he felt that drink had been involved so he hoped that this would be a warning to her in the future and she would become a teetotaler and lead a better life. He also told Mary Ann that they knew she had not been truthful and 'she should try to get a good situation and behave herself or she would be sure to come to something bad.'

1871: Little Jemmy
On Tuesday 18 July, an inquest at the Athenaeum in West Hartlepool with Mr William Gray JP presiding, Mr Settle as coroner and Mr Francis English as jury foreman, was opened into the death of James Nichols, a baby boy of eight months old.

The facts presented at this and subsequent inquests were, that on the afternoon of Monday 17 July, Richard Nichols, the baby's father, returned to his home in Alice Street, Belle Vue, Hartlepool, after his day's work at Richardson's Rolling Mills, to be greeted by his thirty year old wife, Ann, with her calmly announcing that she had poisoned little Jemmy. He shouted to his brother, who lived with them, to go for medical help. His brother returned with Dr Walter Sutherland. The doctor entered the bedroom to see the infant lying on the bed naked,

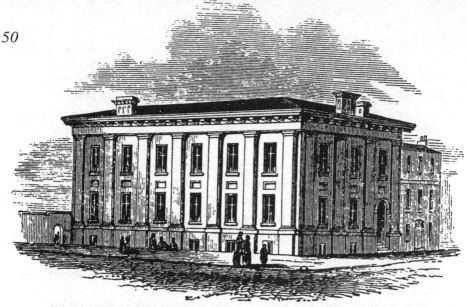

A sketch of the Athenaeum in West Hartlepool as it was when first built in 1852.
Author's Collection

with bedclothes thrown over him. Beside his head was a pillow with what looked like a burn hole in it. His hands, upper chest, neck and the lower part of the face were a dark brown colour. His lips were livid and the inside of his mouth, cheeks and tongue were white and corroded. The doctor determined that the child had been dead at least two or three hours and he thought that some kind of acid might have been poured into the child's mouth and by instinct his hands would have been scorched as they were lifted in resistance. Richard and the doctor then proceeded to the police station to report what had happened. The police returned to the house with them and arrested Ann Nichols.

The Mission Church in Bellvue, Hartlepool. Pattison's Pictures, Bowes Museum.

Mr Gray JP instructed that a post mortem should be carried out, Dr Sutherland and a Dr Mackechnie did this and their findings confirmed that sulphuric acid causing asphyxia and severe shock had been the cause of death. Internally, the baby's lungs, kidneys, liver, gullet, larynx and intestine were discoloured and corroded; the stomach was collapsed with part of it reduced to a gelatinous state where the contents had escaped into the abdomen. The doctors collected nearly a tablespoon of a dark substance from the abdomen. Because of the severity of the damage to the child's body, and the evidence of a burn to the pillow that was beside him, the doctors concluded that about an ounce of sulphuric acid had been poured, undiluted, straight into the child's mouth.

Once the doctor's evidence had been heard, other witnesses were called. The policeman, Sergeant Scott, who attended the scene, produced three bottles that had been found in the rear yard of the property, apparently kept by Mr Nichols for experiments as he had been studying chemistry for twelve months or so. The bottles were labeled 'Laudanum-poison', 'Oil of Vitriol-poison' and 'Spirits of Hartshorn'. Three of the Nichols' neighbours, Sarah Demaine, Margaret Morrisy and Elizabeth Broadbent had gone into the house while the police were being sent for. On seeing the blackened state of the

Nineteenth century bottles of poison similar to the ones found in the Nichols' yard. The Author

baby's face, they guessed that some sort of poison had been administered and asked Ann Nichols, who was crying and very distressed, whether she had given the wrong bottle by mistake, Ann replied:

> *No, I gave it the right bottle. I don't know what I have done it for. I wish I could bring the baby back again. Such a feeling came over me all at once, I didn't know what it could be when I did it, I wish I could bring Jamsey back.*

She carried on to say that at the time she could have done the same to the others. She had two more children, the eldest five years old, who were out playing at the time of the murder.

The neighbours stated that Ann seemed to love her children but had mentioned a few weeks earlier that she thought her husband was having an affair with a French woman in Middlesbrough but did not seem unduly concerned about it and did not seem at all depressed.

The jury at the final inquest brought back a verdict of wilful murder and on 12 December 1871 she appeared at the Durham Winter Gaol Delivery. The same witnesses gave evidence, along with a Dr Samuel Gourley, who had examined Ann on 25 July. He told the court that she had a peculiar shaped head, which he found to be compression to the centre part of the skull. Ann had told him this had been caused by being pitched out of a spring cart many years previously. He stated that this would have caused a weakened intellect that would have been further reduced by suckling her infant and may have caused her to have hallucinations. Because of this evidence and her very evident remorse, Ann Nichols escaped the death penalty but was found guilty of killing her child while in an unsound state of mind and she was ordered to be detained at Her Majesty's Pleasure.

1878: Elizabeth, John and William Barret

Within a day of each other, after a week-long illness in February of 1877, Elizabeth Barret, aged fifteen months, and John Holt, aged four and a half years, both died and were buried in the churchyard of the Holy Innocents at Low

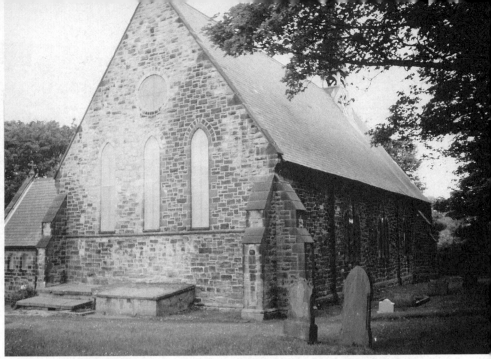

St James' Church in the village of Coundon. The Author

Spennymoor. They were the children of William and Hannah
Barret. In 1978 they had another child, William. When William
was three weeks old they moved from Coundon near Bishop
Auckland, to live at Wingate with William Heaton, a coal
miner, and his wife Sarah.

On 19 January, the first night of the move, William Heaton
told his wife to wake the parents to draw their attention to the
fact that their baby was crying incessantly. Sarah woke them
with some difficulty because Hannah took laudanum so was in
a deep sleep. William Heaton heard no more until the
following morning when Hannah Barret came downstairs and
pronounced that the baby was dead.

Sarah Heaton, Hannah and William Barret were all arrested
and kept in custody at Castle Eden when it was found the baby
had died from opium poisoning.

An inquest was held at the beginning of February at the
George and Dragon Inn at Wingate. Hannah's mother, Elizabeth
Holt was called as a witness. She had been the mother of ten
children, of whom four had died in infancy. Elizabeth was
asked if she had ever given her daughter any medicine for the
children. She said no, but when she had stayed with her

The site of the George and Dragon Inn *at Wingate in 2002, now a doctor's surgery and chemist.* The Author

daughter once, had found a bottle on a window-sill of what she took to be a soothing syrup, but on smelling it, threw it on the fire. When asked why she had disposed of it, she replied that it 'smelt odd, like cinnamon' and that when she was told William had been poisoned, she had asked Sarah Heaton if she had given the baby a drop of laudanum to quiet him because he was crying that night. Sarah replied that she had not given the baby anything. William Heaton stated that he had not seen anyone give any medicine to the baby.

The coroner mentioned that there had been a complaint from a person from Spennymoor on the treatment of the Barret's other two children, but this could be discounted because it related to that branch of the case, and not to William's death. He then instructed the jury that although opium poisoning caused death they had to decide whether it was administered with the intent to kill, by accident or to soothe. If they could not decide they must return an open verdict. The jury agreed that it was accidental and the three prisoners were released from custody.

The church of the Holy Innocents has been demolished but the gravestones of children remain.

A week later the bodies of the other two children were exhumed by order of the Secretary of State. This inquest was held at the *Vulcan Inn*, Low Spennymoor.

An agent for the Prudential Assurance Company stated that Elizabeth Barret had been insured and upon her death her father had claimed the £2 due. The father had been a member of the Ancient Order of Oddfellows and in consequence had also received £2 from the society on her death.

The whole case rested on the evidence of the analytical chemist who examined the bodies. He stated that the organs were badly decomposed and that he could find no evidence of poison left in either one. It was suggested to him that because the children, before death, had both been violently sick, perhaps the poison had been purged from their systems. He agreed that this was highly probable.

The jury had to go by the medical evidence, and although they agreed that the deaths were suspicious and the parents showed gross carelessness, there was not enough evidence to bring in even a verdict of manslaughter. They were found not guilty. Before they left, the coroner told them that they had narrowly escaped being sent to Durham for trial and he hoped that if they had more children in the future they would spend any money they might have on the well being of those children and not on drink.

It was reported later that Hannah and William Barret had looked quite unconcerned throughout the whole proceedings.

The Victoria, *Spennymoor in 2002. There were numerous inns here in the nineteenth century.* The Author

1885: Bertha Dunn

Sarah Dunn was the daughter of a farmer living at Burnhill, near Middridge. Sarah was seventeen and her illegitimate daughter, Bertha, was sixteen months old.

One morning in May, Sarah's parents went to Shildon leaving their daughter and little Bertha at the farm. Sarah was seen about an hour later crossing a field near the farm heading in the direction of Heighington Railway Station. Richard Nelson, a railway porter, saw her arrive at the station and board a train for Darlington. She was carrying two parcels, but there was no child with her.

Sarah had then carried on to Richmond to the house of her aunt. When asked about Bertha, she at first said the child had

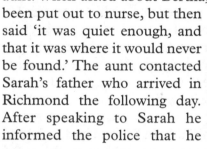

been put out to nurse, but then said 'it was quiet enough, and that it was where it would never be found.' The aunt contacted Sarah's father who arrived in Richmond the following day. After speaking to Sarah he informed the police that he

The Unicorn hotel, Richmond in 2002 with plaque depicting the history, where Sarah Dunn was questioned. The Author

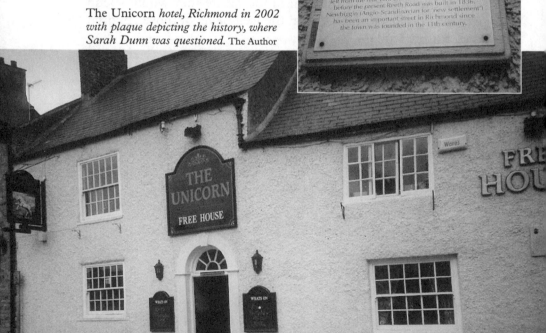

thought she had killed Bertha. The police searched the field near the farm where Sarah had been seen before she boarded the train and it was not too long before they found some loose soil. On digging the soil away they found the body of the little girl. She was lying face down in about a foot of muddy water and on her back were several large stones. The medical examiner found that death was due to asphyxia. Police Constable Graham found Sarah with her father at *The Unicorn* hotel in Richmond and took her into a private room to speak to her. Sarah began to cry and her reply to the constable was:

> *My father behaved very mean to me since I have had the child and what could I do? It would have been hungered to death and it had an easier death than that.*

PC Graham then asked her if she was admitting her child was dead, she answered yes. He then took her to the police station and in the presence of her father and aunt, charged Sarah with murder.

At the inquest, which was held at Auckland Police Court, she was found guilty of wilful murder and was committed for trial at the Durham Assizes.

Her father wept throughout the trial as Mr Milvain, who was acting in Sarah's defence, stated that girls of such a tender age should be better protected by the law and it was Sarah's seducer and betrayer that had committed a foul deed by leaving her in the predicament she was in. Sarah sat with her head in her handkerchief and did not utter a sound.

On 18 July 1885, the jury returned a verdict of guilty but with a plea for mercy. The judge donned his black cap and spoke to Sarah:

> *Sarah Dunn, the jury have discharged their very painful duty with a sense, I have no doubt, of sorrow, but still they have found a verdict, the only verdict with which their consciences could justify. It is one in which I regret to say I entirely concur. I cannot find it in my heart to say one word to add to the misery which this horrible moment must bring to you and those to whom you are dear, and those whom I trust are dear to you. The recommendation for mercy which the jury have*

made will be forwarded to the proper quarter, but it rests with the Secretary of State and not with myself to say what effect shall be given to it. Murder has been done and undoubtedly and unquestionably a cruel murder has been done on a helpless and unthinking child. For that crime there is but one punishment, but one sentence, and that sentence is now my sorrowful duty to pronounce upon you, and that is you be taken from the place where you now stand to the place from whence you came, and from thence to the place of execution in the prison in which you are confined, and that there you shall be hanged by the neck until you are dead, and may the Lord have mercy on your soul.

Sarah was taken from the dock still with her head in her handkerchief, as she reached the interior of the prison she broke down and her grief was pitiable. She was placed in a cell set apart for women who were condemned to death and a female warder remained with her night and day. The execution was to take place on Monday 3 August at eight in the morning.

Immediately after the trial a petition was begun to try to have the capital charge reduced to a minor offence and the Darlington Board of Guardians sent in a plea for mercy because of Sarah's youth and circumstances. On 27 July, Whitehall replied that the Secretary of State had overturned the death penalty and Sarah would instead serve life in penal servitude.

1885: Metcalfe

One Saturday morning in June, Mrs Castle heard a knock and opened the front door of her lodging house in Northallerton. She was shocked by what confronted her. Standing on the step was her eleven-year-old nephew, Metcalfe, who she had not seen for some years. The boy was poorly clad, his hair was long and matted and his feet swollen to twice the normal size. Scabs and sores covered his body and he was crawling with vermin.

The story he told his aunt upset her greatly. Metcalfe said that his mother, who was Mrs Castle's sister, had married a blacksmith from Northallerton, by the name of Waring. Soon

The police station in Church Road, Stockton. Cleveland County Council, Libraries and Leisure Department.

after the marriage, his mother had died and Waring had moved to Stockton. There were another two boys in the house who were Waring's brother's and sister's children. These boys were treated well but Metcalfe was made to sleep in an outhouse in the back yard. He was given no boots and hardly any clothes to wear, was fed scraps like an animal and the two boys occasionally beat him. After four years of this treatment, Metcalfe made his escape. Remembering he had an aunt living in Northallerton, he had made his way there to find her.

Mrs Castle took the boy to South Stockton police station where he was subjected to a searching examination. Metcalfe's story varied slightly when told a second time. The boy told the police that he slept in a back room, not an outhouse, but there was no bed, so he slept on the floor. Other than this, the story was the same as told to Mrs Castle.

The police went to Waring's house and found the back room clean and tidy with a comfortable bed made up. They interviewed the neighbours who said they frequently heard the boy crying as if being punished and that he did not take his meals with the rest of the family.

The conclusion the police arrived at was, because the boy had suffered obvious abuse and neglect from Waring and the two youths, the room had been cleaned out and a bed put in to divert suspicion when he had run away. There was, however, not enough evidence to charge Waring. Mrs Castle took Metcalfe to live with her, and threatened that if the police did not prosecute Waring she would do it herself.

Nothing more was recorded on this case, so one can assume that there was a happy ending for at least one victim.

Chapter 7

The Defenceless and the Innocent
1857-82

1857: A Tailor's Intent

J ohn Foster was a merchant tailor working for Foster and Routledge, tailors and outfitters, of High Street, Stockton. Charles Blenkinsop, a carver, owed Foster money for clothes he had purchased. The firm had obtained a judgment in the county court for the money Charles owed, so his wife, Rachel, borrowed 5s (25p) to pay some of the debt. She went to the back door of Foster's business premises at about 7 o'clock in the evening. Foster invited Rachel in and told her to sit down. She explained that she had brought some of the money and would try and pay the rest as soon as possible. Rachel then asked for a receipt. Foster told her he would send it or she could come back in the morning but Rachel told him that Charles had insisted that she bring the receipt home with her. Foster then began chatting, saying it was a pity that a respectable looking woman should be married to a man that would not pay his debts and he could send Charles to prison. Rachel started to feel worried

High Street, Stockton in the nineteenth century. Author's Collection

The corner of High Street and Little Brown Street in 2002, where Foster's business premises were situated. The Author

and decided not to wait for the receipt, so she got up to leave. Foster jumped between her and the door, still chatting away. He then turned the key and locked the door, put his arms around her and asked for a kiss. Rachel refused and begged to be allowed to leave but Foster shoved her against the wall and raped her.

When Rachel was eventually allowed to leave she ran home and told her landlady what had occurred, she was advised to find Charles and tell him. She found her husband playing bagatelle in a public house and he took her to the police station.

John Foster was charged with rape and assault and tried at Durham Quarter Sessions. It was stated that when Rachel went to the police station, her clothes were disheveled but there were no marks of violence upon her person. She said that she had screamed throughout the attack. The back door of Foster's business premises opened flush onto Little Brown Street and was only six yards (5.5m) from High Street. Both were busy streets at that time in the evening. There were dwelling houses on either side of the business premises, but although neighbours were questioned, nobody had heard Rachel scream. It was pointed out that Rachel had no receipt to prove that she had even visited Foster and that he had the power to send her husband to prison.

Foster was acquitted on both charges. Who was telling the truth? Only Foster and Rachel knew.

1873: Mary Butterwick

Mary was an elderly lady living in Church Street, West Hartlepool, above the offices of Turnbull and Young, solicitors. Her son-in-law was a book traveller and was expected to return one evening from his latest business trip on the train due in at eleven thirty that night. The elderly lady and her daughter, Mary Farndale, went to the front door to look out for him. When they walked down the entrance passage, Mary went to turn the gas down on the light and accidentally turned it off. Her daughter left Mary in the passage and walked to the railway station to meet the train. As Mary stood in the darkened doorway, a man came up to her and asked the time, she replied that she did not know, at that the man seized her by the waist, dragged her into the passage and kicked the door

Church Street, West Hartlepool where Mary Butterwick lived. The opening to the left leads to the railway station. Author's Collection

to shut it, but it remained slightly ajar. He grabbed her by the throat and threw her down on the floor. She shouted as loud as she could but then could remember no more as she must have passed out. When Mary's son-in-law, Robert, and her daughter returned they saw the door ajar and heard the old lady crying for help. On pushing the door open, in the darkness they could just make out someone lying on the floor, thinking it was Mary, Robert bent down to assist her when he grabbed hold of a man instead. He kept hold of him and asked what he was doing, the man replied that he was not doing anything and broke away from Robert and ran off. Mary's arm was badly bruised and her nose was bleeding. Robert went for the police and they caught the man at the back of George Street. The man was a Jamaican, William Travers, who was visiting West Hartlepool from Manchester.

His story was, that when he asked Mary Butterwick for the time she had become agitated because he was a coloured man. She then took a fit and he was about to assist her when Robert grabbed him and threatened to knock his head off. When asked why he had run off, he said it was because being coloured, he would get blamed for something anyway so he thought it wise to run away.

Since the night on which the offence took place Mary had been quite ill but as there were no witnesses to an actual rape, the lesser charge of aggravated assault was brought and he was sentenced to four months hard labour. Travers was then further accused of stealing a lady's dress belonging to Jane Dove from a clothesline in Alma Place, with the intention of selling it. While the evidence was being heard Travers became violent and banging his fist down on the front of the dock, shouted that if a dead body was picked out of the dock he would be accused of murder and, if he had a loaded gun he would prefer to be shot than standing where he was.

The bench then added another two months hard labour to his sentence for his outburst and the theft of the dress.

1874: The Rape of Mary Ward

Christmas, a time of good will, eating, drinking and celebration, but for Mary Ward it meant terror, pain and death.

Mary was a woman of forty years of age who, on having left her husband, made her living travelling the countryside hawking small articles, singing and begging. On Christmas Eve 1873, she called at the doors of several houses in Carlin Howe, near Brotton, trying to sell her wares and make a few shillings. Mary liked a drink and with a little money in her pocket she called into a public house in the village that was frequented by the miners who worked around the area. She became quite drunk and as she staggered out into the street was surrounded by a group of miners who had seen her in the public house and decided to have a little 'fun' with her. They pushed her about, threw a pail of water over her and knocked her to the ground.

Three of the men, Joseph Carter, James Fleming and Henry Shaw then dragged the woman to a nearby field where she was raped. Her screams were heard in the village but no one rendered her any assistance.

On Christmas morning, Mary's body was found at the bottom of the shaft of the Lofthouse Iron Company's mine at Carlin Howe.

The post-mortem revealed that Mary's spine, skull, both legs and one arm were fractured and the other arm dislocated. The examiner thought that these injuries were sustained when

York Prison, now part of the Castle Museum. The Author

she 'fell' down the shaft. Severe bruising to the face and other parts of her body were thought to have occurred before death.

A confession by Fleming and Carter stated that they were present but only Shaw had committed the rape. At the York Assizes in March 1874, Fleming and Carter were found not guilty and walked free. Shaw was found guilty and sentenced to ten years penal servitude for rape.

Did Mary, after the attack, wander confused and in pain to the opening of the shaft and fall, was she dragged there still alive or carried there already dead? There was never any mention of murder, perhaps because Mary was a beggar and therefore unimportant.

1882: Sins of the Flesh

Charlotte Henderson, a little girl of five years old, was playing in Prince Park, Liverpool with Ann Sims who was eight, Jane Sims, who was ten, her brother and some other children when a dark complexioned, unshaven man in a grey suit standing on the grass near the fountain holding an open umbrella, spoke to them. The man asked one of the boys, Alexander Henderson, to go and get him a box of matches. Waiting until the boy had left on the errand and the other children were a little distance away, the man asked Ann, Jane and Charlotte 'to come and sit beside him under his umbrella and play at summerhouse.' Ann replied that she did not want to, so the man said he would give them a penny if they would. Charlotte replied that she did not want a penny whereupon the man pulled her to him, laid her down on the grass, put his hand over her mouth and according to both Ann and Jane's description, committed rape. Ann ran to find a policeman but without success and when she returned Charlotte was standing up and the other children had returned. The man then left the park. Ann saw the same man the following day in Devonshire Road near the park, wearing a different suit and a top hat.

Charlotte, on returning home, was said by her father, Louis, to be 'in a greatly injured condition.' He went for the police who found the man in the park the following day wearing the dark suit and top hat that had been described by Ann.

On questioning, it turned out the man was Patrick Pacifious

St William's Church, Darlington in 2002. Patrick Wade was priest of this parish from 1878 until 1882. The Author

Wade, a Roman Catholic priest from St William's Church, Barton Street in Darlington. He said he was on holiday and did not wish to be detained as he had to return to Darlington to officiate the following Sunday. He also said that he had been on a drinking spree and could not remember what had taken place. The matches that Alexander had been sent for were found in Wade's pocket. On investigation it was found that following Wade being in the park, he had spent that night at a house of ill repute.

A doctor had examined Charlotte just after the event and found her to be torn and lacerated. Eight days later an eminent surgeon was then asked to examine the child and his findings matched those of the doctor.

The trial was held at the Liverpool Assizes and the two medical men were asked whether the injuries had definitely been caused by rape or could they have been caused 'just' by an indecent act. Neither of the doctors could say for certain either way.

The prosecutor wanted to bring in other evidence, which was probably the Sims sister's versions of what had taken place, but the judge deemed it unnecessary and on the medical evidence, thought that the more serious charge of criminal assault should be dropped and an indictment on the lesser charge of indecent assault should be brought. This was done and Father Wade was found guilty of the lesser charge, the judge imposed a sentence of two years penal servitude with hard labour. He never returned as parish priest to St William's Church, Darlington.

Chapter 8

A Murder at Barnard Castle
1860

A tenement in Galgate was the scene of an all too common drink related crime. The house was rented by William Stokeld, who in turn sub-let the ground floor. Moving from Middlesbrough, Sarah Dixon and her children, Sarah's uncle Thomas and his partner Mary Ann Wilson had rented the rooms in May. Thomas worked as a sawyer on the South Durham and Lancashire Union Railway works.

They had all lived peaceably in the house for about five weeks until one Saturday in June. It was pay day, and Thomas had handed most of his wages over to Mary Ann. They both then went out separately. Thomas returned very drunk about one o'clock on Sunday morning and finding that Mary Ann had not returned, he went back out. Mary Ann came in about two o'clock, also very drunk, and fell asleep on the bed beside Sarah and her children. Thomas returned again at four o'clock and fell asleep.

The following morning Thomas went out early and Mary Ann left after she had eaten breakfast. Returning about noon, she went upstairs to speak to the landlord and then collected an empty bottle and went to Borrowdales to have it filled with rum. When Mary Ann returned with the rum, she took a cupful up to the landlord. When she came downstairs, Mary Ann offered a drink to Sarah, which was refused. After continued refusals, Mary Ann, who by now was drunk, got angry and threw a cupful of the rum at Sarah. Just at this Thomas came in, also the worse for drink, and asked what the mess on the floor was. Mary Ann told him that one of Sarah's children, Georgy, had spilt some water. Thomas called Mary Ann a liar and punched her with his closed fist. He then sat down to have his dinner, threatening Mary Ann the whole time

Galgate in the nineteenth century. Elijah Yeoman, Bowes Museum

Barnard Castle in 2002. The Author

that he would make sure she was unfit to work the following day. When Thomas finished his dinner, he hit Mary Ann again, locked the front door from the inside, telling Sarah and Ann it was at their peril if they opened it. He then went to lie down on his bed.

Mary Ann, thinking Thomas was asleep, crept over and unlocked the door. Sitting on a chair beside the front door, she started calling Thomas names. Suddenly, he jumped off his bed and shouted that he was not asleep and had heard the abuse. Thomas locked the door again and then knocked Mary Ann off the chair with his fist. He reached down and lifted the poker from the side of the grate and struck her with it on the head using immense force. Thomas then commenced kicking Mary Ann with his hard navvie boots. Sarah shouted at Thomas to stop but he threatened to do the same to her. She ran upstairs for the landlord and then unlocked the door and ran out into the street screaming for help. When Sarah returned, Thomas was gone and the house was full of neighbours looking in horror at the badly disfigured face and head of Mary Ann.

The blow from the poker had caused instant death, so Mary Ann would not have felt the ensuing kicks. The police went in search of Thomas, who had been seen running out of the town. PC Weldon of Greta Bridge arrested him the same night in the woods of Brignal Banks. On being transferred to Barnard Castle police station, Thomas asked if Mary Ann was dead. He then said he was sorry and it was all through drink.

The jury at the inquest found Thomas guilty of wilful murder. This verdict was overturned at the Durham Assizes and he was sentenced to life imprisonment for manslaughter.

A nineteenth century poker, which made a formidable murder weapon.

Chapter 9

The *Pennyman's Arms*, North Ormesby 1860

Margaret Spring had been the proprietress of the *Pennyman's Arms*. Margaret was a widow who took in lodgers to supplement her income. One of her lodgers was John Dodds, a man of dissolute habits and given to excessive drinking. It was suspected that Dodds was Margaret's 'fancy man' and that they lived together as man and wife. Whatever the situation, it was common knowledge that Dodds treated Margaret with the greatest contempt and disrespect.

Mary Haggerstone worked as a charwoman for Margaret and recalled an incident that had taken place in November 1860. Dodds was very drunk and started using bad language towards Margaret. She picked up his ale from the table and threw it onto the fire, telling Dodds he was mad with the drink. Margaret then said she would not take any more of him and he must find lodgings elsewhere. Dodds hit Margaret, knocking

North Ormesby in the nineteenth century, where the Pennyman's Arms *was situated.* Author's Collection

her down and then continued beating her about the head and face. Margaret managed to struggle to her feet but Dodds grabbed her by the neck and violently began kicking her on the legs. Knocking her down again, Dodds knelt on Margaret's stomach and kept hitting her. Mary ran upstairs and called one of the lodgers to come and help, which he did. Dodds vowed vengeance on the whole house and then left.

Margaret never recovered from her injuries. She could not lie flat to sleep and had to be propped up with pillows and needed assistance to walk. No doctor was called in until towards the end of December. A week later, on Christmas Eve, Margaret died.

Because of the evidence of Mary Haggerstone and others that had witnessed John Dodds being violent towards Margaret, he was arrested and charged with murder.

George Coates, the Middlesbrough surgeon who had attended to Margaret just before her death, carried out a post mortem. His testimony was that when he attended Margaret, she had not told him about the beating. He found her ankle to be swollen and he thought that this and her illness were due to indigestion and congestion of the liver. He therefore prescribed remedies suitable for those complaints. When the doctor attended Margaret a second time, she was complaining of pain in her side so he advised a strong liniment. He did not suspect there was anything seriously wrong.

The doctor's post mortem on the body showed no signs of external injury but of course any bruises inflicted six weeks before, would have by now healed. On removal of the scalp there was an effusion of blood from the brain. Dr Coates and his assistant, Dr Young, both felt that this was the reason Margaret had died. They found that the heart and lungs were slightly diseased but not enough to cause death. Neither doctor could say for certain that a blow or a fall six weeks previously could, or could not, have been the reason for the damage to the brain. Although Margaret had died from effusion of blood they were not prepared to say how that effusion was caused.

The jury retired and after twenty minutes returned a verdict of not guilty and John Dodds was discharged.

Chapter 10

God's Truth
1861

James Whitelock had worked for many years as a clerk for the firm of Messrs Hodgson and Todd, solicitors of Hartlepool. In February of 1861, his whole life changed. The Reverend Joseph Armstrong, minister of the Primitive Methodist Church at Hartlepool took out a prosecution against Whitelock for extortion.

Margaret Redfearn was a distant relative of Mrs Armstrong and worked as a servant for the family. She had been keeping company with Whitelock for some time. On 22 February Margaret handed Armstrong a letter written and signed by Whitelock. The contents were an accusation of a rape against Margaret that had supposedly taken place in January. The letter made mention to 'a wolf in sheep's clothing' and then a threat to make the issue public unless there was some

The Primitive Methodist Church, Hartlepool where Joseph Armstrong was vicar in 1861. The church was eventually demolished. Cleveland County Council, Libraries and Leisure Department

monetary compensation paid. Armstrong took the letter immediately to some of the more influential members of his congregation, then placed it into the hands of his solicitor, who advised him to make a charge against Whitelock.

A trial at Crown Court was set. On the morning that it was due to take place, Armstrong received a summons from Margaret Redfearn charging him with rape. The magistrates dismissed the accusation as entirely groundless.

As the case began, the prosecutor for Armstrong made the point that the case came under two statutes. One passed in the reign of George IV and one in the reign of the present majesty (Queen Victoria). The first was that it was a felony for one person to write to another person charging him with a crime that was punishable by transportation, with intent to extort. The other made it a felony to write a threatening letter for the purpose of obtaining money without any reasonable or justifiable cause.

Armstrong's evidence was, that the morning before he had received the letter he had returned from the country at nine in the morning. Whitelock and Margaret were in an unseemly position on the sofa in his study. Armstrong had told Margaret that her services were no longer required because he felt that this was not fitting behaviour. Armstrong stated that the accusation was in retaliation for him dismissing her. He also stated that once Whitelock knew that Armstrong had put the case in the hands of a solicitor, he came to him and said he would withdraw the accusation. This was done in front of a witness, a borough magistrate by the name of Mr Hunter. Armstrong's reply was:

> He was prepared to take action in this matter and free himself from the imputation that had been cast upon him by the prisoner in his letter. He did not wish to put him to trouble or to do him any harm as he still had, thank God, the spirit of Christ to forgive.

Armstrong refused to accept the retraction because of the insinuations that had been directed against him. This had resulted in Whitelock's committal by the magistrates to take his trial.

In answer to Armstrong's evidence, Whitelock answered:

Your shocking hypocrisy is unparalleled. I neither can nor will retract what I said in my letter. A cloud is gathering, which will soon clap like a thunderbolt above your head.

The defence counsel called Whitelock's employer, Mr Edward Hodgson who testified to the excellent character of his employee. Mr Waters, chief constable of the Hartlepool police, also testified to Whitelock being of excellent character.

The magistrates pointed out that it was strange that the rape had supposedly been committed in January and yet the letter was not written until Margaret had been dismissed from Armstrong's employment.

The magistrates summed up the case to the jury. They then instructed that if the jury thought that Margaret Redfearn had invented the story and told Whitelock and he had believed it, then the jury should acquit him. If they believed that the rape had taken place then they must also acquit. If, however, they thought he had tried to extort money without any justifiable cause, the jury must find Whitelock guilty. The jury retired and after an hour's deliberation returned a verdict of guilty with a recommendation to mercy because of Whitelock's previous good character.

His Lordship then addressed Whitelock, saying that his crime would normally have received a long term of penal servitude. Because of his previous good character and the recommendation to mercy he would mitigate the punishment. Whitelock was then sentenced to eighteen months hard labour.

Chapter 11

The Hart Lane Murder
1864

Matthew Hodgson lived on a small farm at Hart Bushes, sometimes known as South Wingate. He was the father of nine children and in 1864 was sixty-five years of age. Matthew often went for a drink at the *Raby Arms* at Egypt on the outskirts of Hartlepool because one of his daughters, Esther, worked there as a domestic servant.

One fine Saturday afternoon in March, Matthew was having his usual drink when his daughter, because her father was quite fragile and there were a few rather suspect looking men in the bar, asked her father to give her some money, that she knew was in his possession, for safekeeping. He pulled out £4 in gold as if to hand it to her, but then changed his mind and

The Raby Arms, *Hart Village in 2002.* The Author

St Mary Magdalene Church, Hart in 2002. The Author

returned it to his pocket. At around 4.00 in the afternoon, when Matthew left to head for home, one of the men asked where he lived. A youth that was a cousin of the Hodgson's answered that it was Hart Bushes. Shortly after this the man left the public house.

At about 5.30 pm that afternoon, the Reverend William Harrison, vicar of Hart Church, was driving with Mr Dryden in his conveyance along the main highway between Sunderland and Hartlepool, when they saw a tall dark man coming towards them. A little further on they came upon Matthew, barely alive, lying in the middle of the road. The spot, known as Slidden Bank, was very near to the village of Hart on a part of the road that was between two high banks sheltered on either side with hedges. The spot was concealed from the view of anyone who might have been nearby. The marks on the turnpike showed that a struggle had taken place and underneath Matthew's head was a pool of blood. Matthew was taken to Hart and remained unconscious for about half an hour. On coming round he said,

*There were three of them, I left Hartlepool this afternoon and
three men followed me. One of them felled me. I do not know
them but my daughter does. I had £4 in gold in my right-hand
trouser pocket and some in the other. I afterwards found the gold
I had was gone but the silver remained untouched.*

After making this statement, which the Reverend had written
down, Matthew lapsed back into unconsciousness. He never
spoke again and on Monday evening he died from a fractured
skull caused by a heavy blow to the head.

Immediately after Matthew was found, two navvies were
charged with highway robbery and violent assault. One of the
men was Joseph Charlton, who was about sixty years old and
came from Hexham, and the other was Joseph Skelton, from
Cumberland. Soon after they were locked up, a friend of
theirs, Wilson, arrived at the police station looking for them so
he was also detained. All three denied the charges, with Wilson
saying he had been at Newcastle at the time and could prove
it. When Charlton was apprehended he was holding a large
stick that was thought could be the weapon that had been used
to hit Matthew. Another large stick was later found near the
scene of the crime, this one with blood and white hairs

*Once the village of Hart Bushes where Matthew Hodgson had a farm, only a few
ruined buildings in the fields now remain.* The Author

adhering to it.

An inquest was carried out at the Hartlepool Town Hall by the county magistrates to determine whether the three men in custody were guilty. Esther, Matthew's daughter was the first to speak, she explained her worry about her father having money on his person and walking home alone. Besides asking him to leave it with her, she had also asked him if he would leave it with Jane King, landlady of the *Raby Arms*. She said that throughout the conversation about the money, Charlton was listening and then had left straight after her father and returned about an hour later looking for his friends. They, by this time, had already left. She could remember four men sitting drinking together that day but Wilson was not one of them. The next witness was Margaret Denton who said she lived at Hart Warren and on the Saturday in question she had been on her way to Hartlepool when she saw a man lying on a hill near to the arch bridge that led to the North Sands. On her return she saw the same man leaning against some railings at the side of the road holding a large stick in his hand. She then saw Matthew Hodgson walking along the road towards Hart and as she walked up the embankment to go along the railway she saw the man with the stick following Matthew, but, she said, none of the men in custody were the man she saw. Next to speak was Henry Dodds who had passed Matthew whilst walking about a mile from Hart. As Dodds continued on his way he saw another man a few hundred yards further on. He thought he looked rather suspicious but he did not fit the description of any of the prisoners. Francis William was a foreman at Messrs Richardson and Sons, and was lodging at Egypt along with the prisoners. He stated that Wilson had been at Newcastle that Saturday and there were many people who could vouch for that. On this evidence the three prisoners were released.

A second inquest was carried out a few days later, and by this time the two other men who had been drinking in the public house that Saturday had been found. One was Henry Butters and the other was Adam Curry, both navvies lodging at Egypt. Curry had returned to his lodgings on the Saturday afternoon according to his landlady 'in a very flurried state.' He had told her he was catching a train for Sunderland. When

Hartlepool Town Hall where the inquest on Matthew Hodgson's murder was held.
Cleveland County Council, Libraries and Leisure Department

he did not return to work on Monday the police set out to look for him and he was apprehended at Stockton. None of the witnesses were able to identify the two men as being the ones seen on the road that fateful day. Both were released for lack of any evidence. The jury returned a verdict of 'wilful murder by persons unknown.'

The coroner felt he should submit the case to the Home Secretary with a view to having a reward offered for information leading to the conviction of the perpetrator of the crime and that if a Queen's Pardon should be given to the two who did not actually wield the stick perhaps they would come forward and give the name of the one who did. A point that was brought up before the court that was dismissed, was that Matthew had said his daughter knew the three men, did he mean the three that were in the public house that day as everyone had assumed, or could they have been men that she was acquainted with otherwise?

Chapter 12

The Hermit of Seaton Snook
1866

Where the Seaton Carew Golf Club and course is now situated was once a windswept, gorse-covered tract of land close to the sea that was used for grazing livestock. In March 1866, a new resident arrived to make his home on The Snooks. He had an old carriage, which he had secured to the bottom of a boat, not much larger than a coble, as his habitat. Inside he had a fireplace, seats, a small table and shelves that were, surprisingly, filled with books on law and folders of papers. He paid the lord of the manor 17s 6d (88p) for the freehold rights to live on the land and purchased a small boat for fishing at the cost of 10s (50p) and 'a buggy' to collect wood, sea coal and anything else he could find on the shore, for 7s 6d (38p). His age could not be determined as his features were partially covered by a long shaggy beard and

Kirkleatham Hall, part of the Kirkleatham estates. The hall is now in use as a museum. The Author

The windswept Snooks at Seaton Carew where the old hermit dwelt. The Author

shoulder length hair, and his clothes were old fashioned, ragged and dirty.

Every Sunday the hermit attended Holy Trinity Church at least twice and the villagers of Seaton Carew came to know him. Although he was polite and pleasant to speak to, and also obviously very intelligent, the villagers thought that perhaps his mind wandered a little as he talked of owning part of the Cleveland Hills and Kirkleatham Hall. The hermit was given gifts of food, which he accepted gratefully as his main diet consisted of shellfish and fish that he caught himself. He said that he had come from Newport and that his name was Timon; the villagers dubbed him 'The Hermit, Timon of the Tees.'

Timon settled down quite happily in his wild, lonely domain, spending many hours reading his beloved collection of books until one day in June when everything changed for him. He returned from his daily fishing trip to find his 'boat house' on fire. Of course, there was plenty of seawater near at hand, so he was able to extinguish the blaze quickly but all his books and papers were destroyed and a few of his possessions

Holy Trinity Church, Seaton carew in 1888. Pattison's Pictures, Bowes Museum

Cockle women in the nineteenth century. Pattison's Pictures, Bowes Museum

A modern-day 'boathouse'. The Author

were missing. Local people thought it was the work of the West Hartlepool cockle women who came to collect the shellfish around Seaton Bay.

Timon had other ideas, he insisted that the person or persons who had caused the damage had done it on purpose. His story was that the papers that were in his possession proved that he had the right to become the landed proprietor of the Kirkleatham estates and they had been burnt to stop that happening. He had been in the process of studying the law to see the best way of going about his claim. Timon said he was one of twelve children born out of wedlock and that their father, the lord of the manor of Kirkleatham had told his wife about his infidelities when she was on her death bed.

The hermit repaired his 'boat house' and remained living at the Snooks until 1873. Whether his story was true or just the ramblings of a lonely, inoffensive man and whether it was one of his rival siblings or the cockle women who had committed the act, the fact remained that he had little enough to start with and everything he treasured was destroyed in the cruel act.

Chapter 13

Conflicting Evidence
1866

With the coming of industry, Middlesbrough suddenly blossomed from farmland to town in a very short space of time. By the 1840s small, cramped houses were being built to accommodate the workers who arrived in the hundreds. These men were hard working and hard drinking, and with a wage in their pockets they frequented the many public houses and fights and trouble both in the streets and in the home were a common occurrence.

A policeman on the beat in Middlesbrough at one o'clock in the morning heard a disturbance coming from a court in Stockton Street. He could hear someone quarrelling and a woman screaming but because of the locality the sounds were coming from he was not unduly alarmed and walked on by. On returning a little later, with the disturbance still going on, he decided to investigate. He entered 65 Stockton Street, the house of James Donaghey, to see a strong looking young man lying dead on the floor. There was blood all over his head that had come from two deep wounds. The man was James's son, Lawrence Donaghey, who was twenty three. The woman who had been screaming was Lawrence's mother.

The couple told the policeman that they had gone to bed about eleven that night and a little while later Lawrence had knocked at the door so his mother had got up and let him in. She was not sure if he was drunk at the time but he was not injured. Something had awoken them at about 12.30 in the morning and on lighting a candle it was to find their son dead. The mother said she had not had a drink that night.

Nine people occupied the small house, Mr and Mrs Donaghey, their daughter, four sons, two of whom were very young, and two lodgers who were cousins to one another. Owen Collins, one of the lodgers, told the police that

Cramped houses on a narrow lane that were built for workers and their families. Author's Collection

Middlesbrough Town Hall in the nineteenth century where the inquest was held on the death of Lawrence Donaghey. Author's Collection

Lawrence was the only lad to help support the family and he had never heard wrong words pass between them. Later, at the inquest held at the Middlesbrough Town Hall, he changed this statement and said there were frequent quarrels, sometimes about Lawrence drinking and sometimes about him not passing over enough money. On the night in question, Owen said the father had gone to bed with a good drink in him and the mother had also had a glass or two. When Owen heard the commotion and came downstairs the father was not dressed but the mother was fully dressed, sitting on the floor cradling Lawrence's head in her arms and screaming.

A neighbour, Samuel Crowther, who lived at 69 Stockton Street, said he had been woken to shouts of murder, at the time he only heard the voices of two women. He went down to the yard and listened at the door where he said he could hear the mother and elder sister shouting; both of them said 'Don't murder poor Larry it will be a bad job.' Samuel then went back upstairs and watched from his window. He saw no one enter or leave the house until a good hour later when Mary Donaghey, Lawrence's sister, went to Susan Bartley, who lived in the same court, to say Larry was dead and could she please come to the house. Samuel also said that there were often disturbances, usually between the mother and Lawrence. Susan Bartley went to the house and saw only the mother, sister and the body of Lawrence, the father was not in the room. Susan said there was often quarrelling between the family although she did not know what they argued about, it was usually the mother's voice she heard.

On the Sunday night, Lawrence had been first in the *George and Dragon Inn*, where Mr Elson, the landlord, said he had left just after nine with a good drink in him. He had then gone to the *Liberal Beerhouse* in Stockton Street. At about ten that night the landlord, Mr Taylor, seeing the young man was well intoxicated, asked his nephew, James Miller, to see Lawrence home. James took him towards his home where, he said, a woman he thought to be Lawrence's mother, came up to them in the road with a jug full of some liquid in her hand. James had hold of one of Lawrence's arms, the mother took hold of the other and led him indoors. The mother said something to her son in anger but James could not understand what was said. James then returned to his uncle's beerhouse and went to bed.

The cap Lawrence was wearing that fateful night was examined for blood, there was none, the furniture in the house was also examined to see if he could have fallen on something that would cause the head wounds, but again, nothing.

At the inquest the medical examiner stated that death had occurred from a fractured skull and the injuries had been applied with a heavy instrument such as a poker or a kick from a boot.

The jury decided that because of the conflicting evidence they would have to return a verdict of 'murder by some person or persons unknown'. No one was ever prosecuted for the crime.

Chapter 14

A Fatal Affray
1866

etween Hartlepool and West Hartlepool, which were once separate towns, was Middleton, known to the locals as 'no man's land.' It was here one Saturday evening that three noticeably drunken men accosted a platelayer, Joseph Hardman, who worked for North Eastern Railway, as he crossed the rail track on his way to work. Joseph had been called out to do an emergency repair to a bridge. He had called into the cabin of John Hudson, who was a gatekeeper and signalman for the same company, to pick up a hand lamp. He was swinging the lamp by his side, when three men, obviously trying to cause trouble, told him to keep it away from them, as it was dazzling them. Joseph told them to be off, at which one of the men began to swear at him. Once again Joseph told them to be off and go to their homes. This angered the men and all three attacked him. John Hudson heard the commotion and went to Joseph's assistance. A rather lengthy battle took place before the three rogues retreated. When they had gone and the two men were getting their breath back, John told Joseph that he had a terrible pain in the back of his head where one of the men had struck him with a heavy stone. Joseph also had a few bruises to his face and head but as the injuries did not seem serious to either man, they bid each other goodnight and went their separate ways.

John made his way to the dock ferry and telling one of the boatmen what had taken place, he repeated to him that his head was very painful. He crossed on the ferry from Middleton to West Hartlepool and was not seen again until found lying unconscious about seventy yards (64m) from the ferry landing. The police conveyed him to Church Street and some of John's friends met them there and took him to his home in Union

A ferryman rowing a passenger from Middleton to Hartlepool Ferry Terminal in the nineteenth century. Pattison's Pictures, Bowes Museum

The Athenaeum, Church Street, Hartlepool in 2002, now a listed building. The Author.

Place, Stranton. He spoke only once and that was to whisper 'water.' Because of the way he was staggering and then passing out, his wife and friends thought he was drunk. A doctor was not sent for until Sunday morning, but by then it was too late, John breathed his last without regaining consciousness. He was thirty-one years of age and left behind a wife and four children.

The police were told that the name of one of the three men who had begun the fracas was Cowell, they apprehended a John Cowell, but were soon to learn that it was not him but his brother, George Cowell, that had been involved. The other two men were Francis Dunn and William Brown. All three men gave themselves up to the police and were charged with causing the death of John Hudson.

A post-mortem showed John had a broken hand, bruising and a fractured skull that had been caused by a blow with something heavy. The cause of death was a blood clot on the brain caused by the blow. As soon as the results of the post mortem were available an inquest was begun at the Athenaeum in West Hartlepool.

Although the three men giving themselves up to the police and admitting to the affray testified to their guilt, the jury was instructed that they had to decide whether the felony committed was murder or manslaughter. If his death was carried out with premeditation or malice aforethought then it was murder, if it occurred without malice, it was manslaughter. They also had to decide whether John's death was caused by violence and, if so by whose hand.

Joseph Hardman was called as a witness but at first refused to take the oath, saying that he could not swear that the three men that were in custody were the men they had fought with. Joseph at first also refused to pick up the bible, when he eventually did, he did not touch it with his lips, a policeman noticed and the bench sharply ordered Joseph to 'kiss the book.' Eventually it was sorted out and he then related what had taken place on the fateful night. Joseph told how he had managed to fend off the man that was attacking him then go to John's assistance, as two men had him down. One of the men struck Joseph with what he thought may have been a stone then put his arm around his neck and was strangling him. Joseph managed to bite the man's finger hard and when he let go the man ran off. They managed to fight off the other two men who also disappeared into the night. Joseph still insisted he could not identify the three men even though he had been carrying a lamp and must have been able to see them quite clearly.

A seaman whose ship had been moored at a slip nearby on the night of the affray was then called as a witness. He had heard noises that he thought sounded like a fight then saw a man run past the slip crying 'my finger, my finger.' The man had then ran in the direction of West Hartlepool and a few minutes later another man followed the first. The seaman could not identify the men as they were too far away and the night was hazy. At this testimony the coroner asked for a doctor to examine the prisoner's fingers. This was duly carried out and the doctor confirmed that the middle finger on Cowell's right hand had been recently bitten.

The jury retired and after an absence of nearly an hour returned a verdict of manslaughter against the three seventeen-year-olds, Cowell, Dunn and Brown, who were then conveyed to Durham Gaol.

At the Assizes the jury came to the conclusion that all five men in the altercation had been as bad as each other and while the three that were on trial were guilty of manslaughter, there was also a strong recommendation for mercy.

The judge felt that it was not a transaction to cause severe punishment and because of the jury's recommendation for mercy, he sentenced the prisoners to three months hard labour.

Chapter 15

The Shootings at Darlington
1869

S aturday night in Darlington and the beerhouses and inns were packed with hard working, hard drinking men, many of them Irish, employed in the ironworks around the vicinity.

The police were often called to drunken quarrels between the men and this particular Saturday was no exception. A man named William Young was at *Costello's Beerhouse* where there was dancing and singing taking place. Young went into the yard to use the water closet when he saw another man, Thomas Finnigan follow him and aim a revolver at his head. Young jerked to one side and a bullet whizzed past where his head had been a second before. He ran off and informed the police of the event.

Later that night a sergeant and two police officers found Finnigan at the *Havelock Arms* at Albert Hill. When Finnigan saw the police, he tried to pull the revolver from his pocket but it got caught and the officers managed to seize him and take him into custody.

The police were called again to the same locality at around midnight, this time because a murder had taken place. It seemed that an Irishman, Phillip Trainer had gone into the *Allan Arms* at Albert Hill. He left ten minutes later and then gunshots were heard. On the customers going outside they found Trainer lying on the road. A bullet had gone through his left eye, killing him instantly.

The police had great difficulty in extracting information but eventually they apprehended two men, one was Thomas Hanlon and the other a puddler by the name of John McConville, or 'Gentleman John' as he was better known. Both were in their mid twenties and were described as well dressed, superior looking men.

A witness told the police that on the previous Saturday night he had seen McConville and Finnigan whispering to each other. However, the police did not think that the two shootings were related. George Turnbull and his wife Ann, who were the hosts of the *Allan Arms*, said, that on the night of the incidents there had been five or six men in their front kitchen including John McConville and Phillip Trainer, another man came in and struck one of the men in the group. The landlord told them all to leave the premises. Trainer, who was a sober and quiet man, remained for about ten minutes talking to a man named Burns and then he also left. Immediately after Trainer left, a gunshot was heard.

A witness, James Quinn, told the police that while still in the *Allan Arms*, McConville had asked him if he knew a man that was walking through the bar, Quinn replied that the man's name was Burns. McConville then said that Burns was a fighting man but his pal Hanlon could beat him. Quinn said that he thought Burns would beat Hanlon, whereupon McConville had patted his pocket and replied that he had something there that would stop him. When they all went outside, Quinn saw McConville take a revolver from his pocket and fire into the crowd of men that were standing in the street and then calmly walk away.

The police arrested McConville and Hanlon, they did not find any firearms, but when McConville's lodgings were searched they found a revolver cover. It was thought that the revolver found on Finnigan was the same one that had been used to kill Phillip Trainer. An ironmonger came forward to identify the cartridges found on Finnigan and the one used on Trainer. He said they were the same type that he had sold, along with a revolver, to a man giving his name as John Jackson He thought the man he had delivered the firearm to was Hanlon.

Finnigan's story was that he had revolver that a friend wanted to buy; because his friend was drunk, instead of giving him the revolver to try, Finnigan had gone outside and fired it into the air.

At the initial trial of the three men, McConville, Hanlon and Finnigan, there was not enough evidence to implicate Hanlon

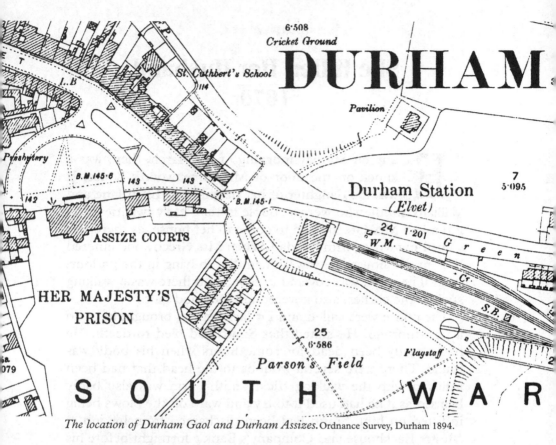

The location of Durham Gaol and Durham Assizes. Ordnance Survey, Durham 1894.

so he was dismissed. Finnigan and McConville were committed for trail to the Durham Assizes, the first on attempted murder and the second on murder.

The jury came to the conclusion that there was no evidence to prove that Finnigan had intentionally set out to kill anyone so he was found not guilty and discharged.

John McConville was found guilty of murder and Justice Lush passed sentence of death. The executioner, William Calcraft, hanged him on 22 March 1869. His was the first private execution to take place at Durham.

Chapter 16

She Killed Her Husband
1870

Early on Sunday morning of 20 March, there was a knock on the door of Mrs Greenwood's house. It was the daughter of her neighbours, Ellen Jane and William Smith, who were a couple in their early twenties. The girl asked Mrs Greenwood to come to her house, as there was something wrong with her dad. When Mrs Greenwood entered the Smith's house she saw William Smith lying in the parlour, dead. The room was covered in blood and there was a walking stick in the corner, also covered in blood and hair.

The police were called and Dr Jackson was brought in to do a post-mortem. He stated that Smith had bled to death. He had already been dead for some hours when his body was found. There were several wounds to the head that had been inflicted with the walking stick. Smith's arm was also badly bruised as if he had used it to try and ward off the blows being inflicted on him. Smith had been discharged from his job at Messrs Backhouse and Company's Bank a fortnight before his death. On the afternoon of Saturday 19 March, Smith had driven about Darlington in a cab, transacted some business, and then gone home. The cab driver said that Smith had not had a drink and was quite sober at that time.

Annie Hart had lived in with the Smiths as a servant for about two years. She said that both her employers drank and they often quarrelled. Smith would often hit his wife and she in turn would retaliate and hit him back. Annie said she was always having to try to make peace between them.

Ellen Smith denied that she had killed her husband saying that Smith had taken his own life. At the inquest, the judge, addressing the jury, said that it was impossible for Smith to have inflicted the injuries he had sustained on himself.

Ellen was found guilty of manslaughter with a

recommendation for mercy because of extreme provocation from Smith.

At the Durham Assizes the jury agreed with this verdict. The judge told her that she had had a narrow escape from being charged with murder. He then sentenced Ellen to ten years penal servitude. At this, Ellen Jane Smith fell to her knees in the dock and wept. She was then led away to her fate by two female warders.

Chapter 17

Did He Fall or Was He Pushed?
1870

George Pinkney lived at Chapel Row, Shildon, and worked as a brakesman at Eldon Colliery. He had been keeping company with a young woman who worked as a servant at the *Sportsman's Arms* in Bishop Auckland and had been there one Sunday evening. He had left about ten thirty that night, and then called in at the *Red Lion* in Newgate Street and drunk a glass of whisky. The servant there said he was neither drunk nor sober at closing time.

In the very early hours of Monday morning Constable Coverdale, stationed at South Church, was called to a cabin in the Tunnel Brick Yard, Eldon Lane by two women, Mary Barker and Jane Craddace. On a long-settle, partly undressed was the body of George Pinkney. The constable searched his pockets, which were already turned inside out, there was no purse but Mary Barker handed over George's watch and guard.

The story that was told to the police was, that on the Sunday night three men were in Craddace's cabin, when Barker and Craddace went for some beer to *Metcalfe's Public House*, walking a few yards behind them was Robert Jefferson. As they passed under the bridge, they saw George lying on the roadside. Finding that he was unable to walk they assumed he was drunk so they carried him into the cabin to let him sleep it off, they then went to buy some beer. At about three in the

Modern brickworks in Eldon Lane, Shildon. The Author

Houses at the brickworks. The Author

morning when he still had not moved, Craddace realised there was something wrong and that George was dying. She called in a signalman who was on night duty at the railway and after he had a look at George, the signalman then went for the police.

The body was taken to George's house where Dr Smeddle was called in to perform a post-mortem. He found that George had a large wound on the top of the head and a severe fracture of the skull. He did not think it could have been caused by an accidental fall but George could have sustained a fracture such as this if he had been pushed violently.

The bridge under which George was found was about twenty-seven feet (8.22m) above the road, at the point where

Shildon Tunnel near to where George Pinkney fell or was he pushed from the bridge?
Author's Collection

the Stockton and Darlington railway crossed Eldon Lane near to the entrance of Shildon Tunnel. On inspection of the site, a pool of blood was found and on the wing of the bridge were nailed footmarks that corresponded with the boots George had been wearing, so he could have been trying to clamber down the bank and lost his footing. The curious aspect of the case was that there were also footprints leading up the bank, and George's purse, hat and handkerchief were never found.

The two women, Barker and Craddace, were considered of questionable character and suspicion was directed at them and the four men who had been in their company.

People crowded the street outside the *Fox and Hounds* in Shildon where the inquest was held. The jury thought that the medical evidence was not specific enough to prove murder and returned a verdict of:

> *Found dead at the roadside with a wound to the skull but how or by what means he came to his death there was not sufficient evidence to show.*

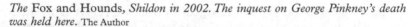

The Fox and Hounds, *Shildon in 2002. The inquest on George Pinkney's death was held here.* The Author

Chapter 18

The Foreign Sailors
1870

Far from their Norwegian home, some sailors were having a night out at the *Golden Lion Tavern*, High Street, Hartlepool. At closing time, as they left the tavern, one of the men, Theodore Thorstensen from the *Louisa Maria*, shouted that he was going back to his ship. Another man, Hans Harsen, alias Charles Brown of the *Albert Frederick*, replied that he was going to stay ashore for a while. Thorstensen then put his hands up in an attitude of fighting and knocked Harsen to the ground. Harsen picked himself up and retaliated by punching his aggressor, knocking him down. On rising, Thorstensen took a knife from a sheath at his side and struck out at Harsen, hitting him in the breast. With blood pouring from his chest the wounded man staggered as far as the *Dock Hotel*, a distance of a few yards, and fell, exhausted.

Southgate in the nineteenth century where the Dock Hotel *was situated.* Pattison's Pictures, Bowes Museum

The Coal Dock Offices in 2002, now part of the Historic Quay. The Author

A number of men that had seen what happened, and going to the aid of the injured man, they carried him to the police station. The police called Dr Rawlings, but by the time he arrived the man's life was beyond saving.

Thorstensen, meanwhile, had run off towards the ferry. The police immediately gave chase and tracing him to Middleton, began a search. They came across a seaman, and on questioning him it transpired that he was from the same vessel as the wanted man and was able to direct the police to the *Louisa Maria*, which was berthed at the coal dock in West Hartlepool. Thorstensen was found lying on his bunk. The police told him to get dressed and then they escorted him onto the deck and searched him but found no weapon. The prisoner admitted to striking Brown, but denied stabbing him. The police then searched the deckhouse and after some time found a sheathed knife stained with blood. The weapon was formidable, being of a dagger shape with double edges and a very sharp point. Thorstensen admitted the knife was his.

At the inquest, at the request of the Norwegian Consul, a solicitor was present to watch the proceedings. Three of the men that were at the scene on the night the murder was committed were called to give evidence. All denied actually seeing the fatal blow struck, although one did admit that the knife found in the deckhouse and produced as evidence was Thorstensen's, as he had seen him peel an orange with it on the previous night. The prisoner agreed that was true, except it had been an apple he was peeling, not an orange. Throughout the inquest, Thorstensen's demeanor remained calm as if he was accepting his fate. He eventually admitted to the stabbing and said he had committed the offence whilst under the influence of alcohol and was very sorry.

He was committed to take his trial at the Durham Assizes on the charge of murder. The witnesses were bound over to testify at the trial.

At the trial, the charge was reduced to manslaughter and Thorstensen was sentenced to three months penal servitude.

Chapter 19

Infanticide
1873-83

1873: West Hartlepool

Walking along the sands one afternoon between Carr House and Cliff House, John Chilton, a seafarer, spotted something that looked out of place protruding from a lofty part of a sand hill. On closer investigation he found it to be the body of a dead infant wrapped in a filthy piece of linen. It was in a shallow hole about six feet above the high tide watermark. He informed the police who conveyed the body to the dead house where it was examined by a surgeon, Rilton Oldham. His findings were that it was the body of a female infant that had been dead some time. The hands and feet were nearly separated from the body and the right arm and face were crushed. His deductions were that the child had been born alive and crushed to death soon after birth then buried in the spot where it was found.

At the inquest held at the *Royal Hotel* in West Hartlepool, the jury's verdict was 'wilful murder by person or persons unknown.'

The houses on the cliff above Carr Sands in 1864.

Normanby High Street in the nineteenth century. The Author

1876: Eston

Annie Elizabeth Parker was seventeen, and the eldest daughter of Eliza and Charles who lived at Swan's Cottages in Normanby. In January of 1876 she was charged with the murder of her new-born female child.

Eliza had thought her daughter to be a little off colour and had asked her if she was in the family way, Annie denied this adamantly. On the evening of 8 January, Annie complained being in pain so Eliza made up a dish of mustard and water for her to sit and soak her feet. Eliza then went to visit a neighbour. On her return Annie was kneeling by the fire and said to her mother that she had gone to the privy and could hardly get back to the house. Meanwhile, the next-door neighbour, Elizabeth Osbourne, thought she heard a noise that sounded like a moan coming from the ashpit (privy) that adjoined hers. She shouted to a neighbour, Elizabeth Walker to come with her to have a look. Taking a lighted candle, the two women went into the ashpit and found a baby girl lying on its face. There were no signs of the baby having been born in the

A privy or ashpit of the nineteenth century. Cleveland County Council, Libraries and Leisure Department

ashpit. They carried the child, which was alive, into Eliza's house where Annie was still kneeling in front of the hearth. Eliza asked if the baby was hers and she answered that it was. Annie was then told to go upstairs to her bed while a doctor was called for. Meanwhile, Elizabeth Walker washed the child and on doing so noticed a mark on the left side of the mouth and that the right arm seemed to be broken.

The doctor arrived and on examining Annie, confirmed that she had just given birth. He then examined the child and found her to be dead. He would not issue a death certificate and told Eliza to inform the police, which she refused to do. The doctor informed the police himself and took the body for a post mortem. The findings were, that one arm was broken and badly bruised as if by a tight grip, a wound at the back of the mouth extended down and had separated the gullet and the windpipe from its structure. A fractured jaw and multiple scratches completed the injuries. In the doctor's opinion, all of the injuries had taken place after birth. Some instrument had been used to cause the injury to the back of the mouth, not a person's hand.

Annie at first said that she had been delivered of the baby in the ashpit and the child had fallen. When the police inspected Eliza's house they found that although there was blood in the ashpit, there was even more on the hearth where her mother had found her. Their conclusion was that she had given birth in the kitchen of the cottage.

At Annie's trial the doctor testified that the injuries could not possibly have been caused by the birth. Annie herself eventually admitted the child was born in the kitchen, but gave no explanation as to how it came to be in the ashpit. The police stated that there were suspicious marks on the ashpit wall, as if the baby may have been thrown against it. No instrument that could have caused the wound to the back of the mouth was found in the ashpit, so the wound must have been inflicted in the kitchen. Even with all this damning evidence against her, perhaps because of her youth, the jury found her not guilty and Annie was at once discharged.

1883: Middlesbrough

Early Monday morning, on 4 June, a baker's boy, Arthur Martin, was doing his deliveries in Middlesbrough, when he noticed a bundle between the railings and the hedge of a garden in Borough Road. He lifted the bundle out and unwrapped it, to his horror he found it was the body of a tiny baby. Arthur stopped a woman that was passing and she went for a policeman. The body was taken to the police station and a medical examiner was called in. His conclusions were that the baby had been born healthy and been strangled immediately after birth. There was a skein of wool in the bundle that matched grooves round the baby's throat.

On enquiry, a man came forward to say he had seen a woman at about five on the Monday morning looking over the hedge where the body had been found. His description led to the arrest of Charlotte Wilde and her sixteen year old daughter, Rebecca. A doctor's examination of Rebecca on 6 June showed that she had given birth about a week previously. Rebecca was indicted for murder and her mother for taking part in the disposal of the child, and they were both sent to stand trial at York Assizes.

Charlotte denied knowing her daughter was pregnant but said that she was 'very ill' on 31 May. There were no witnesses and the prisoner's defender stated that it could not be proven that the child was born alive. The prosecutor then abandoned the capital charge and proceeded with the lesser charge of concealment of birth.

At the conclusion the judge advised that although there was suspicion there was no evidence to justify conviction. Accordingly the jury then acquitted both the accused so Charlotte and Rebecca were released.

Chapter 20

Mary Ann Cotton
1873

The crimes, trial and subsequent execution of Mary Ann Cotton was probably the most notorious case to take place in this area, made all the more infamous because she was Britain's first female serial killer (to be caught) and it was also believed that many of her victims were children.

Mary Ann was born in 1832 in Low Morsley, to very young and poor parents. When Mary Ann was still young, the family moved to Murton where her father met his death by falling down a mineshaft. It would have been the workhouse for herself, her mother and brother if her mother had not remarried, so perhaps that was why Mary Ann had a lifelong obsession with money. When she was sixteen Mary Ann left home and went into service, then, in 1852, she married William Mowbray, a miner. They travelled around England going wherever there was work.

Out of five children that were born in the first four years of their marriage only one survived. The marriage was apparently not a happy one as arguments were constant over Mary Ann's obsession with money. Eventually William took a job aboard a ship that hailed from Sunderland, so Mary Ann moved there to be nearer the dock. Her children continued to die of one form of illness or another. In 1865 William spent time at home due to an injured foot, and within a month he had succumbed to an intestinal complaint. After William's death, Mary Ann picked up the insurance money, then moved to

Mary Ann Cotton.
Reproduced by kind permission of Durham County Record Office, ref: UD/Sea33. Durham Arts, Museums and Libraries

Seaham Harbour where she met Joseph Nattrass. They became involved even though Joseph was already engaged to someone else. Once Joseph's wedding had taken place, Mary Ann moved back to Sunderland. By this time only one of Mary Ann's nine children, Isabella, still survived and she was sent to live with her grandmother. Mary Ann took a job at the Sunderland Infirmary where one of her duties involved cleaning with soap and arsenic. She was well thought of by the staff and patients and soon became involved with one of the patients, George Ward, and, after he was discharged from the infirmary in 1865, they were married. Just over a year later, after a long illness, George died of intestinal problems. Mary Ann moved on once again, this time taking a job as a housekeeper and child minder to James Robinson, a widower. Within a month James's infant son was dead. He turned to Mary Ann for comfort and she soon fell pregnant. Then Mary Ann's mother took ill so she went to care for her, a few days later her mother, who had been on the mend, was dead. Mary Ann then took her daughter, Isabella, back to live with James Robinson. Within just weeks of each other, Isabella and two more of the Robinson children were buried. Amazingly, James, at that time, can have suspected no wrongdoing as he and Mary Ann were married. Their first child was born, but this infant also soon succumbed to illness and died. James belatedly started to become suspicious, not only because of the deaths but because Mary Ann kept pressing him to insure his life. Then he began to receive letters about debts Mary Ann had incurred and his remaining children told him that she had made them pawn valuables from the house. He threw her out and she left taking their second daughter with her.

Now she was on the streets, a way of life that she had always feared. She went to visit a friend and asked if she could leave her daughter there for a few minutes while she went an errand. She never came back for the child so the daughter was returned to James Robinson.

Eventually, a friend, Margaret Cotton, introduced Mary Ann to her brother, Frederick Cotton, who was a widower and had two surviving children out of four. Once a relationship developed between Mary Ann and Frederick, Margaret, who had lived with her brother, soon became ill and died and Mary Ann moved in. She became pregnant once again and not disclosing that she had a husband who was still alive, she married Frederick. She quickly insured him and his two sons. She gave birth to a son, Robert.

Hearing that her previous lover, Joseph Nattrass, was now without a wife and living in West Auckland, somehow she managed to move the family there. Frederick died soon after the move and Joseph moved in as a lodger.

Mary Ann took a job as a nurse to John Quick-Manning, who was recuperating after a bout of smallpox, and she became pregnant by him. Soon afterwards Frederick Cotton's youngest child, Mary Ann's own son Robert, and Joseph Nattrass were all dead. She did not have her own son buried immediately but waited until Nattrass died so they could be buried together (to save money no doubt). Before his death Nattrass had changed his will, leaving everything to Mary Ann.

She was now only waiting to claim the insurance on Frederick's remaining son, Charles Cotton. Mary Ann sent him to the chemist to buy some arsenic but the chemist refused to sell the poison to him. She then asked a neighbour to purchase it for her, which was done, and Charles died soon after.

By 1872, Mary Ann's luck was running out. She had made the mistake of speaking to a government official, Thomas Riley, about placing Charles in a workhouse because he was interfering with her plans to marry Quick-Manning. Riley had told her that he could not go on his own and that she would have to go to the workhouse with him. At this she had replied that Charles 'would go like the rest of them.' Riley met her a few days later and was shocked when she told him Charles was dead. He went straight to the police and a doctor to voice his suspicions. The doctor had attended Charles through his brief illness and had not thought that it was life threatening, so agreed not to issue a death certificate until an inquest had been held. Mary Ann was furious because she could not collect the insurance without a death certificate. The inquest showed no foul play so Mary Ann went to Riley and told him because of his meddling he should pay for Charles's burial.

Mary Ann would probably have gone on to claim many more victims if it had not been for the press. They got wind of the story and as well as being present at the inquest, they talked to neighbours and printed the gossip that alluded to her being a poisoner. Quick-Manning ended their relationship and Mary Ann prepared to move on once more, but a doctor had kept some stomach samples from Charles and on testing them he found arsenic. The bodies of Charles and Nattrass were exhumed and the charge of murder on Charles was brought against Mary Ann. The trial was delayed until after the birth of her child to Quick-Manning on 10 January 1873. The child was taken from her as soon as it was born and given to a couple to bring up as their own.

Because of her pregnancy, a petition was begun on her behalf and signed by ministers, previous employers and others who had found her a patient and caring person, but the evidence at the initial trial held at Bishop Auckland belied what her supporters had seen in her character. Witness after witness came forward to testify to her purchases of arsenic, to

The exhumation of bodies.

the symptoms of the illnesses all being similar and to the apparent good health of most of the deceased shortly prior to their deaths. She was committed for trial to the Durham Assizes where she maintained her innocence but was found guilty of the murder of Charles Cotton and sentenced to death.

Justice Archibald donned his black cap and gave his closing statement:

> *Mary Ann Cotton you have been convicted, after having a careful trial, of the awful crime of murder. You have had the benefit of counsel for your defence and everything that could possibly be urged on your behalf has been said. The jury have arrived at the only conclusion to which they could have come-that you are guilty. You have been found guilty by means of poisoning your stepson, whom it was your duty to have cherished and taken care of. You seem to have given way to that most awful of all delusions which sometime takes possession of persons wanting in moral and religious sense-that you could carry out your wicked designs without being convicted and that you could carry them out in secret: and by means most detestable to all and at which human nature shudders-by means of poison. But it is one which has left most clear traces of guilt. You must seek for your soul the only refuge which is left, the mercy of God and the atonement of Jesus Christ.*

Mary Ann's mother, three husbands, her lover Nattrass, Margaret Cotton, five stepchildren and ten of her own children had died. How many from natural causes and how many were her victims is a secret that went to the grave with her.

Mary Ann Cotton was hanged on 24 March 1873 by the executioner William Calcraft who was known for his 'short drops,' so instead of her death being quick it took over three minutes for her to be strangled by the noose at the end of the rope. She was the last woman in England to be hanged after giving birth.

Chapter 21

The Ginger Beer Seller
1873

Martha Addison was known as an industrious woman, living opposite an works, she made ginger beer to sell to the workers. Martha had originally come from Barnard Castle but had moved in with a man named Charles Dawson at Cleveland Street, Darlington. Dawson already had a wife in Stockton and although he was occasionally employed as an ironworker, his main source of income was from poaching. It was well known to the neighbours that Dawson ill-treated Martha. The house where they lived was also home to three lodgers, two of whom were Patrick Dempsey and Thomas Mullen.

One Saturday evening Martha and Dawson called in to visit a widow, Rachael Newton, who was a friend of theirs. Dawson was already the worse for drink and while in Rachael's house, slapped Martha with the palm of his hand and then left. Martha stayed a little longer chatting to Rachael and then she also left. Dawson returned later on looking for Martha and finding her gone, said to Rachael 'if I light on her again, I'll make her that she'll not run away so soon.'

The three lodgers had left the house with Dawson that evening and went for a drink. Mullen and Dawson went to look for Martha, finding her at the railway crossing at Albert Hill. As soon as Dawson came face to face with Martha, he struck her behind the ear with the flat of his hand, knocking her down. The three of them then went to their house.

Once inside, Dawson locked the door and put the key in his pocket. He took of his coat and waistcoat, lit a candle and then picked up a revolver. Dawson then threatened Mullen, telling him that if he raised the alarm or spoke to anyone about what he was going to do, he would shoot him. Dawson then picked up a bottle and hit Martha with it, she fell to the floor and he threw the bottle at her. It missed and smashed into pieces. Dawson then began kicking the defenceless woman who began to scream. He put his foot over her throat to keep her quiet and kept kicking her in the ribs with his other foot. Eventually, Dawson seemed to tire of that and instead jumped up and down on her stomach a few times. At that there was a knock on the door from Dempsey, Dawson let him in then kicked Martha again before picking up a coal rake and striking her in the ribs with it.

Mullen and Dempsey had stood by not saying a word, but at this act Dempsey said to Dawson that he had killed Martha. His reply was that she was not dead. Still holding the revolver, Dawson picked up an earthenware pot full of dirty water and threw it over Martha's face, then, bending over her he smashed the pot into her face knocking out several of her teeth. Dawson then seemed to have finished his violent attack as he told Mullen to get him some clean water to wash her face.

Mullen dashed out of the house and to the police station. When Superintendent Rogers accompanied him back to Cleveland Street at about twenty past eleven he found Martha lying on the floor with her head on a bolster pillow. Her face had been washed but there was blood on her hand and running out of her ear onto the floor. Broken plates were scattered around, chairs were upturned, the back of an armchair was broken and the place was in a state of utter confusion. There were two guns and two pistols in the room, which the superintendent took possession of. He then commenced proceedings to apprehend Dawson.

About two-thirty on the Sunday morning, the police spotted Dawson's dog. On following it they found Dawson sitting in a house not far from his own home. He offered no resistance and admitted to killing Martha.

Martha had not partaken of any alcohol and the two lodgers who witnessed the brutal attack testified to it being completely unprovoked. Dawson was found guilty of murder and sentenced to death. His execution took place at Durham on 5 January 1874.

Chapter 22

Until Death Us Do Part
1873-89

Sadly these accounts show that sometimes a woman's life was not held in particularly high regard. It was perhaps not so much accepted, but certainly in most circumstances tolerated, that a husband could chastise his wife or partner to keep her in hand. If the chastisement went too far and resulted in her death, especially if alcohol was involved on either side, the perpetrator might walk free or the coroner would instruct the jury to bring in a verdict of manslaughter, so the sentences could be quite lenient. Only in recent years have 'domestics' been considered a matter of police concern.

1873: Mary Ann Kennedy

At the Durham Assizes, George Rutherford, an engineer who was aged twenty-four, was charged with feloniously wounding with intent to murder Mary Ann Kennedy on 14 December 1872 at Stockton.

The two had been 'keeping company' for a while and on the night the crime was committed they had gone for a walk. Rutherford had apparently told her that if he saw her in the company of a friend of his named Pace, he would 'knock her soul out.' When they were about to bid each other goodnight Rutherford had suddenly aimed a blow at her head, she put up her hand to ward off the blow. Because it was a cold night she was wearing a muff and as she stopped the blow she felt something sharp penetrate the muff and cut her hand. Rutherford then aimed towards her head again and she became extremely frightened and ran into the road to call for help. A young man named Carter heard her and ran to Rutherford, managing after a struggle, to take the knife from him. Another man who was in the vicinity had seen the whole episode and heard Rutherford say that he would swing for her and she deserved all she got. Mary had a bad cut to her hand and the knife had gone through the back of her head cutting an artery and causing her to lose a large amount of blood. She was lucky to be alive. Rutherford's family, on giving evidence, stated that he had headaches and hallucinations and sometimes they had to give him drugs to calm him down. They also said that an aunt in the family had been insane for the last twenty years.

The jury decided that Rutherford knew what he was doing and was completely sane at the time of the attack but although they found him guilty they gave a recommendation for mercy. He was sentenced to five years penal servitude.

1881: Catherine Chambers
William and Catherine Chambers moved to Lawrence Street in West Hartlepool in mid January 1881, by February Catherine was dead.

Sophie Paxton, who lived at number four Lawrence Street, became friendly with Catherine and would call in to see her every morning after William had gone to work. Usually the door was unlocked and she would go in and waken Catherine. On Friday, 4 February at about eight thirty, Sophie went to the house and finding the door locked and the blinds drawn, she knocked but received no answer. She returned in the early

Church Street, Hartlepool where William Chambers was arrested. Author's Collection

afternoon and finding the door still locked, became worried and went to fetch Catherine's brother-in-law, Thomas, who lived nearby in Pilot Street. He forced his way into the house and they found Catherine, unconscious, lying on her bed with her face buried in the pillow. There was a little blood on the sheet but none on the pillow. Her day clothes were lying over the end of the bed slightly torn but not bloodstained. A doctor was sent for and Sophie went to find Catherine's sister. When Dr Biggart arrived he found two wounds, one that was fairly superficial above the left eyebrow and a deep one on the right ear. There was also bruising on the head and face including black eyes but none of the external injuries looked to the doctor as though they were life threatening. The doctor used a stomach pump and tried to revive Catherine in other ways but to no avail, she remained in an unconscious state.

Charles Averill, a police inspector, was passing at the time and had followed Curran and Sophie into the house. He saw a hammer lying on a table, a poker, tongs and coal rake lying about on the floor and in the kitchen and pantry the pieces of a broken earthenware bowl. When his superior arrived they collected these items and took them to the police station. On inspecting the items, one of the broken shards of the bowl had a mark that looked as though it could have been blood. Inspector Averill knew the couple well, he had often seen Catherine with black eyes and she had complained to the police on several occasions about William assaulting her. William said that he hit his wife because she was always drinking with other men.

The police went looking for William and found him walking down Church Street, where they arrested him for unlawful wounding of his wife. Upon being asked if he knew what condition his wife was in he answered that he knew all about it and it was due to her being drunk the night before and falling on a basin she was using to bake bread. He said he had left her in bed that morning thinking she would be all right.

Dr Biggart had stayed with Catherine throughout the rest of that day and into the following, still trying to revive her, but, early on Saturday morning she slipped away without regaining consciousness. The charge against her husband was now murder.

Dr Biggart and two other medical examiners carried out a post mortem. Besides the bruising to the face and head there were also marks on her knee and wrist and an old burn to her face. She had not been drinking and the cause of death was a blood clot on the brain, which they felt could not have been caused just by her own bodyweight in a fall. In the opinion of the three doctors either Catherine had been hit with something or pushed very violently and with the injury that she had sustained she would not have been capable of getting undressed and into bed herself, yet according to her husband that was what she had done.

At the inquest, which was held at the West Hartlepool Police Court, the first witness was Bridget Farran, a neighbour of the Chambers, who stated that she had seen Catherine under the influence of drink on a few occasions, but the last time she had seen her she was sober. That had been on the Thursday when Cathcrine was baking bread, using the earthenware bowl that had been found in the house and was now produced as evidence in the courtroom.

The next witness was Robert Bluekart who lived with his family next door to the Chamber's house. He told the court that he had been woken by the clock striking three on Friday morning and shortly afterwards had heard William threatening to knock his wife's head off and Catherine shouting 'Oh no, don't hit me again.' Alfred Bluekart, Robert's son, said he had been woken at about the same time as his father, by what he thought was the sound of a cup breaking. He had shouted to his mother who was in the adjoining bedroom 'Mother they're quarreling again next door.' Alfred attended Ward Jackson School and had gone as usual on Friday and had not told his mother about the breaking noise he had heard until he returned home.

Alfred's mother, Sarah, had knocked on Catherine's door on Thursday afternoon at about three o'clock to ask for help in wringing out some sheets she had washed, they hung the sheets to dry and Catherine went indoors. About an hour and a half later Catherine went to Sarah and asked where she might obtain something to dress a burn. Sarah told her she

The Blacksmith's Arms, *Stranton, 2002.* The Author

might get some ointment from the *Blacksmith's Arms* but did not ask about the burn or whether it was recent but thought that Catherine was quite sober at the time.

The last witness was Margaret Curran who stated that her sister had not been drunk since New Year but she did like a glass or two. About two years previously Catherine had a fall when she was drunk and had burnt the side of her face.

The jury considered all the evidence and after careful consideration decided that whether the earthenware bowl had been the cause of her injuries or not, she had met her death by violence and William Chambers should be tried at the Durham Assizes on a charge of manslaughter. He was granted bail of £20 for himself to appear and two sureties of £10 each.

At the Durham Assizes, the defence insisted that Catherine had fallen onto the bowl herself. The jury came to a verdict of not guilty as no witnesses were present to prove that it was not an accident.

1887: Margaret Louigi

Margaret, whose maiden name was Boyle, had been married in 1873 at the age of nineteen, to Ambrosina Louigi, a mariner. She had lived at North Shields with her husband until he went to sea in 1879, she then received a 'kind' letter from him that was sent from New Zealand and never heard from him again.

Shortly afterwards she met William McNally, a labourer. They moved in as tenants on the ground floor of twenty nine Ropery Lane, Hartlepool in about June of 1887 when Margaret was aged thirty-three. According to neighbours, theirs was not a happy relationship, although Margaret was quiet and a good housewife, McNally would often be seen and heard assaulting her.

At lunchtime on 14 September, Mr and Mrs Shave the landlords, who lived on the floor above the couple, heard McNally shouting 'Get up you old cow or I'll kick your guts out, where's my dinner?' Margaret had replied, but the only word the Shave's could make out was 'oven.' There were a few loud thumps that sounded like kicks and then Margaret cried out 'Oh Bill you've done me at last.' John Shave did not interfere because he said he was not a strong man and would not be able to stand up to McNally. Sarah Harrison, a neighbour from next door had heard the commotion and came running in and said to McNally 'Are you going to kill the woman for nothing?' McNally swore at her and told her it was none of her business; he then threatened to kick her too. Sarah went back into her own house and a few minutes later she saw McNally leave, presumably to go back to work.

About an hour later Mrs Shave heard Margaret call her from the bottom of the stairs. On Mrs Shave reaching her, Margaret fainted into her arms and then slid down onto the floor. Mrs Shave shouted for Sarah Harrison and between them they managed to get Margaret into her bed. When McNally came home at teatime he was in a foul mood and was going to strike Margaret again. Mrs Shave intervened and told him that she thought Margaret was in a bad way. McNally asked Margaret what was the matter with her and she replied in a feeble voice that he had jumped on her stomach and had finished her. He replied that it was not her stomach he had kicked but her hip. She lingered on until Thursday, complaining continuously that McNally had kicked and jumped on her. Eventually on Thursday afternoon a doctor was called, but ten minutes after his arrival Margaret died.

At the inquest the doctor stated that Margaret's body was covered in bruises, there was a mark on her skull, in his opinion, from a recent blow to the head and the cause of death was a ruptured spleen caused by violence. McNally pleaded not guilty and said he had not caused the ruptured spleen but admitted to kicking her on the head. He went on to say that she had been in poor health for a long time and his sister, who was present in the court, asked to speak and said the same. All the neighbours, however, stated that Margaret had seemed in fine health until this last assault. They also all agreed that there had been arguments between the pair prior to this incident that had ended in McNally using violence against Margaret.

The jury was taken to view the body and when they returned they were instructed that they must either bring a verdict of manslaughter or murder. They brought in a verdict of manslaughter and McNally was sent to trial at Durham Assizes where he received a sentence of ten years penal servitude.

Margaret was buried on Sunday 18 September in Hartlepool cemetery with very few mourners present besides her parents and the priest who conducted the service.

1899: Grace Hartley

The Crown Court at the Durham Assizes was packed for the trial of Frank Garvey, a hawker. He was accused of murdering Grace Hartley at Buckton's Yard in Darlington on 25 March. She had died of peritonitis of the bowel. The prisoner's demeanor was calm and he was seen to turn round and nod at a young girl in the gallery.

Grace had formerly been the wife of Peter Hartley, a tinner at Malton, who had died. Grace had met Frank Garvey, he had moved in with her and her daughter, Annie. They lived in a miserable room in Buckton's Yard. The local authorities had since closed this and the other rooms in the area.

Neighbours to the deceased were called as witnesses and all agreed that on 25 March at about nine in the evening they heard Grace stumbling up the stairs and assumed she was probably drunk. A little later Garvey came in singing and shouting. The neighbours heard Grace tell him to be quiet and then heard Garvey shouting abuse at her. Screaming was heard and then a bump as if something had fallen.

Annie Hartley, who was thirteen, was then called on to give

Buckton's Yard, Darlington in 2002, where Grace Hartley died. The Author

evidence. She told the court that she and her mother had been staying in Darlington a fortnight, prior to that they had lived in York. On the night in question her mother had a 'little sup' but not much. Garvey had come in noisily and Grace had told him to get out and threw a salt pot at him. Garvey struck her on the face and then on the mouth. Grace fell with her back partly on the table and Garvey had taken a running kick at her and loosened her teeth. Annie said that then he took off his shoe and 'brayed' Grace's side with it. Garvey left and then returned in the early hours of the morning and began assaulting Grace again. This time he had jumped on her chest saying that 'now she wouldn't be able to eat any more pudding.' The next morning a doctor was called and just before Grace died, she told him that her injuries had been caused by falling downstairs and onto the tap.

Garvey's story was that when he had gone home, Grace had been very drunk, he remarked upon it and she threw a salt pot at him. Garvey struck her across the face with his hand. He did not see Grace again until the following morning when he noticed she had a cut above her eye. Asking her what had happened, she said that she had fallen downstairs and cut herself. Garvey denied striking Grace more than once, saying that Annie did not know what she was talking about as she had St Vitus Dance (fits) 'and that if she were sent for bread she would come back with bacon.'

The prosecution produced a sketch of the stairs and tap where Grace was supposed to have received her injuries. The tap was outside and it would have been impossible to fall onto it from the stairs. The prosecution believed that Grace, even when she was dying, had lied to protect Garvey.

The post mortem showed no external injuries that would have caused death. The medical examiner testified that a severe blow could cause internal injuries without there being any external sign.

The judge directed the jury to find Frank Garvey 'not guilty' and within ten minutes they returned with that verdict.

Chapter 23

The Triple Execution
1875

1875: William McHugh: Barnard Castle

On Sunday 11 March the body of a man was pulled from the Tees near the steps on the south side at Bridgegate, Barnard Castle. He was a labourer by the name of Thomas Mooney who was married with one child. His wife was currently serving a sentence in Northallerton Gaol. Their child was staying with Thomas's mother.

When the body was pulled from the river it was initially thought that Mooney had fallen in the water accidentally as death was from drowning. On closer inspection four wounds above the eyes were found. All had been inflicted while Mooney was alive. His neck was swollen and there was a red mark upon it. The post-mortem revealed that, while none of the wounds could have caused death, two of the more severe ones could have caused unconsciousness. On the wall at the riverside near to where the body was, there was a silk handkerchief. He had some change in a pocket but his purse was empty. Mooney's mother told the police that he had

The bridge spanning the River Tees at Bridgegate. The Author

collected some money for his employer on Saturday afternoon but she did not know how much.

The police proceeded with an investigation. Subsequently, on their findings, they arrested four men, William McHugh, William Gillighan, Thomas Brannen and Teddy Cannarn. A witness came forward saying he had heard Gillighan and McHugh talking in *Dobson's Beerhouse* on Sunday evening. Although no name was mentioned it seemed to refer to Mooney's death. The conversation was about 'hanging the man, being transported for life, stairs and tumbling into the water.' The witness stated that he was sober when he overheard the conversation but could not remember exactly how much he had had to drink at the time.

When Mooney's body had been pulled from the river it was taken to his mother's house. McHugh and four women were present when the body was brought in. One of the women remarked that the cut to Mooney's eye looked as though a knife had caused it. McHugh had answered that it was not a knife but that he knew who had dealt the blow.

It appeared that Mooney had visited his child on Saturday. Then in the evening, he and some other Irishmen had assembled in the house of William Gillighan to have a drink.

Bridgegate, Barnard castle in the nineteenth century. Author's Collection

Bridgegate in 2002. The houses that once came right down to the river bank are now gone. The Author

Early on Sunday morning a neighbour had heard arguing from the house but could not hear what was said. Later on that day Brannen had gone to Gillighan's house and asked Gillighan's sister, Margaret, if she had found his handkerchief as he had left it on the table. It was nowhere to be seen. It transpired that it was Brannen's handkerchief that was found near the river.

At the ensuing inquest Brannen and Cannarn were discharged and Gillighan and McHugh were charged with murder. They admitted to the police that they had a scuffle in Gillighan's house on Saturday night, but said that Mooney had then left. Brannen and Cannarn told a different story. Their version was that after the scuffle in Gillighan's house they had left to go to their lodgings. The door was locked so they headed for another house. As they passed Gillighan's yard they saw three men. Gillighan had Mooney by the right arm and McHugh by the left. They were on the wall by the river. McHugh was telling Gillighan to throw him into the water. Gillighan refused so McHugh threw Mooney in. Knowing Brannen and Cannarn had seen him, he told them to be quiet about what they had witnessed.

At the Durham Assizes, Gillighan was cleared of the charge. McHugh was found guilty and sentenced to death. He protested his innocence to the end saying that it was Brannen and Cannarn who had carried out the murder.

1875: Elizabeth Pearson: Gainford

Elizabeth Pearson was twenty-eight and married. Elizabeth had her own house, but she was living in the house of James Watson to look after him. James was seventy-four and had been ill. A lodger by the name of George Smith also lived there.

On 15 March George Smith went to Jane Pearson, who was Elizabeth's mother-in-law, saying that James Watson was ill. When Jane arrived at the house James was in bed and seemed to be in agony. Elizabeth was sitting by his bed holding his wrists, probably to stop him convulsing. Jane went downstairs to find some brandy, but when she returned James was dead. His head was thrown back, his teeth were clenched and his body was taut. Dr Homfrey had been treating James for his illness. On his last visit he had been going to prescribe some pills, but Elizabeth had suggested that a powder would be easier for James to swallow. When the doctor was advised that James was dead, he became suspicious as the illness had not been life threatening. He carried out a post mortem and took some of the stomach and some of the liver and sent them to Leeds School of Medicine to be tested. Strychnine was found, enough to kill a feeble, elderly man.

Elizabeth was arrested on suspicion of poisoning James. It then transpired that, on two occasions, a month previously and on 2 March, Jane Pearson had bought packets of *Battles Vermin Killer*. John Corner, the grocer that they were purchased from said that Jane had told him they were for Elizabeth, as the house was infested with mice. Jane said she had been asked by Elizabeth not to tell anybody, as her husband did not like mouse powders. The police searched the two houses, but found no trace of mouse powder. Elizabeth denied any knowledge of the powder.

Immediately after James's death, Elizabeth had taken all of his furniture to her own house. At the inquest the prosecution stated that this was the motive for the crime. George Smith attended the inquest but then disappeared and was not seen in Gainford again.

At the Durham Assizes Elizabeth was found guilty and sentenced to death.

1875: **Michael Gilligan: Darlington**

John Kilcran lived in Church Street, which ran from Park Street to the Skerne opposite St Cuthbert's Church. This was a poor locality and squalor and dirt were rife. Kilcran was a forty-two-year-old Irishman who worked as a builder's labourer. He had a wife and four small children to support.

Easter Sunday 28 March, a time of peace and rejoicing, but not for Kilcran. He was walking along Park Street, seemingly minding his own business, when seven men approached him. One of the men, Michael Gilligan, pulled something out of his pocket, went up to Kilcran and struck him with it. Kilcran fell to the ground and another two of the men rushed up to him and kicked him about the head. All seven then walked away leaving their victim lying in a pool of blood. A witness called

The River Skerne, Darlington in 2002. The Author

St Cuthbert's Church, Darlington in 2002. The Author

Durham Gaol and Assize Court in 2002. The Author

Marwood the executioner who introduced a more humane form of hanging. Brian Elliott

the police. Kilcran had multiple bruises and a deep wound above his eye. He died of his injuries a few days later. The police arrested James Durkin, James Flynn and Michael Gilligan. All three protested their innocence of any involvement in the incident.

The post-mortem showed that the wound above his eye had been inflicted with considerable violence. It was thought that a hatchet or a sharp piece of iron had been used. Witness after witness came forward to testify to the three prisoners being involved. At the Assizes Durkin and Flynn were found guilty of manslaughter and sentenced to fifteen years penal servitude. Gilligan was convicted of murder and sentenced to death.

All three prisoners protested their innocence to the last. These totally separate crimes ended up with common denominators. There was a recommendation for mercy for all three as they had been of previous good character. The plea was rejected by Whitehall on 31 July. William McHugh, Elizabeth Pearson and Michael Gilligan were hanged at Durham on the same day by the same executioner. The hanging took place on 2 August 1875 and the executioner was William Marwood. The bodies were left hanging for an hour before being cut down.

Marwood was a Methodist and deeply religious, believing that even criminals deserved a humane death. He introduced the 'long drop' to England. This meant that as soon as the split trapdoor opened, the carefully measured length of rope and the body weight would snap the vertebrae and cause asphyxia. Thus the person being hung would be rendered unconscious before death instead of the slow strangulation of the 'short drop' that had been used previously.

Chapter 24

Robbery and Assault
on the Highway
1876

After attending the theatre and heading home to Nelson Street at just after eleven o'clock on the night of 28 August, and on nearing the *Queens Hotel* in Mainsforth Terrace, West Hartlepool, Sergeant Robert Page of the Durham Royal Artillery Volunteer Corps and his friend Thomas Cass saw several men standing on vacant ground. They recognised four of them. They were James McGlynn, Patrick Karney, Michael Garvey and Michael McNiff. Garvey approached them and asked for a match, Cass went to take one from his pocket when Garvey suddenly hit him and knocked him down. As Page went to his assistance, McGlynn hit him and then six or seven men proceeded to kick and punch the pair. They then ransacked his pockets taking 13s 6d (68p) and a small key. Page then felt a boot on his face and in his mouth and he passed out. Meanwhile, Cass had managed to get up and ran home. He returned a few minutes later with his wife and Mrs Page, as they approached the men all ran off. Page was taken to a house in nearby Lynn Street where he remained unconscious for a good few hours. The injuries he had sustained were severe. His nose was badly broken as were most of his teeth. His face was covered in bruises and there was a deep gash on one side and his body was also badly bruised.

The four men whom Page and Cass recognised were all known to the police and were soon apprehended and locked in separate cells. A police officer heard them talking to one another and saying that they might get six months or five years in Durham for the incident and if they could only get out they would 'fettle' Page and Cass. The hunt went on for the other men involved in the attack but they were never apprehended.

The four's predictions of what their sentence might be was well short of the actuality. They were charged with highway robbery and violence and sentenced at Durham Assizes, not only to penal servitude but also to flogging. They were each to serve fifteen years in Durham Gaol and to receive twenty-five strokes of the cat-of-nine-tails. Another man, Brown Harrison who had also committed an act of robbery with violence on John McCormack at Rowlands Gill in September was sentenced at the same time. He was ordered to serve twelve years and to be given twenty-five strokes of the cat's tail.

On a Tuesday morning in December, the flogging ladder was set up in the south wing of Durham Gaol. McGlynn was the first to have his sentence carried out. Leather coverlets were placed around the hands, drawn up to the utmost limit of the arms and then fastened round the wrists, and in this way the prisoner was secured to the ladder with his body stretched so it could not contort. The ladder was then moved to the south-east wing and Karney and Garvey were given their punishment. The following morning, McNiff and Harrison received their twenty-five lashes. It was reported that the four screamed throughout the flogging and their suffering was severe.

Chapter 25

Her Father's Daughter
1876

Georgina Clark Pattison was only sixteen when she died by her father's hand. John Pattison was a painter and lived with his daughter, her stepmother and a lodger, Fenwick Trotter, at 6 Havelock Street in Stockton. Pattison was well thought of in the neighbourhood although he was known to have a violent temper. The stepmother was considered a gentle and kindly soul.

Georgina had been with a neighbour, Fenwick's sister, Mrs Trotter, one Saturday. They had met as they left their homes and had walked into Bishopton Road together and then onto the High Street. Mrs Trotter was going to the butchers and Georgina to the market. They parted company at the old church. Later on that night Georgina arrived at Mrs Trotter's house to borrow some coals for her father. While Mrs Trotter was in the yard at the back of the house talking to her lodger, Walter McNeal and another man, Thomas Pollard, who had his hand on Georgina's shoulder, Pattison arrived. He started shouting at his daughter that if she did not get home he would lift her. Mrs Trotter took him into the sitting room and told him that she had not wanted to give Georgina the coals in front of Thomas Pollard, as he was a stranger. McNeal and Mrs Trotter's sister went to fetch the coals and Pattison left with Georgina behind him carrying them in a bucket. Mrs Trotter was worried that the girl would get a thrashing because of the mood Pattison had been in, so she and her sister followed them. They looked in at the Pattison's window where a blind only came halfway down and saw Georgina lying on the floor with her father standing over her shouting for her to get up. The girl was crying as if she was afraid so Mrs Trotter knocked on the door and shouted that if she heard any more noise she would call the police. Mrs Pattison, Georgina's stepmother came to the door and said Mrs Trotter could come into the house if she 'would hold her tongue.' Mrs Trotter told her that if she saw something she did not like she most assuredly would not 'hold her tongue'. At this the stepmother shut the door and locked it. Mrs Trotter and her sister waited about fifteen minutes but there was no more noise. While they were there, something was put across the bottom of the window so they could not see in. They did, however, see the gas turned down low and then, a few minutes later, turned high again.

Fenwick had been in the sitting room when Pattison came home with Georgina. He heard a noise like a knock, and as he stood up and turned towards the door, he saw Georgina fall, her father behind her holding a long sweeping brush shouting at her that he would teach her to stay out late. Georgina's stepmother came downstairs to see what the disturbance was and that was when Mrs Trotter knocked on the door. Fenwick asked Georgina if she was all right and she answered that her head hurt. He then went to bed and heard no more that night.

The following morning the Pattison's knocked on Fenwick's bedroom door asking him to come downstairs. Georgina was lying on the couch in the kitchen, where she always slept, looking extremely ill. Fenwick immediately went for medical help. By the time they returned to the house her father was sitting on the kitchen floor cradling Georgina's head in his arms, she was dead from the effects of a fractured skull.

When the police asked Pattison what had happened, he said Georgina had fallen when she had been carrying a bucket of coals into the house the night before. She had then got herself undressed and into bed where, the following morning, he had found her nearly dead. Pattison was then arrested on suspicion of his daughter's murder.

Several hundred people lined the streets for Georgina's funeral and when Fenwick and Mrs Trotter made their appearance the crowd started to boo and hiss at them, only the appearance of the police stopped the enraged mob from starting trouble. The general feeling was that Pattison had done nothing wrong, he had only chastised an erring daughter.

At the trial, the skull of the dead girl was handed round for the jurors to inspect. The medical examiner stated, that although the skull was thin, the fracture had been caused by something heavy, not by just a fall. Fenwick Trotter, on giving his evidence stated that he had seen Georgina fall and her father holding the sweeping brush, but he had not seen him hit his daughter with it. Mr Fawcett, who defended Pattison, stated that any father, whose daughter had stayed out late and then been found with a stranger's arm on her shoulder, would have been irritated and Pattison had only been thinking of his daughter's welfare if he had acted with such violence towards her. The presiding judge agreed with that statement and ordered the prisoner to be removed from the court until he had considered the case. Pattison was recalled to the court and told that the judge had decided that the death of his daughter was accidental and the case was therefore dismissed.

Chapter 26

The Child in the Park
1884

Henry Bolckow, a wealthy industrialist, gave Albert Park to the people of Middlesbrough. It was opened in 1868 and had boating lakes, cricket and croquet areas, a maze and a bandstand, an ideal place for the children to play.

Saturday morning, 21 June, the weather was fine, so eight year old Mary Cooper, the second youngest of a family of five, left her parent's house at 66 Waterloo Road to go and play in Albert Park. She stopped and knocked on the door of 34

Location of Waterloo Road where Mary Cooper lived at number 66, and Albert Park where she went to play. Ordnance Survey, Middlesbrough 1913.

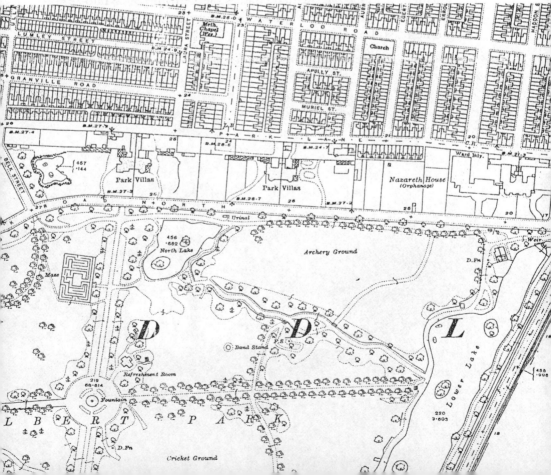

Waterloo Road to call for her friend, Kate Jordan. Kate was not quite ready to go out as she had her boots to clean first. Mary was going to wait for her but Kate's brother, Edward, told her to be off, so Mary headed for the park alone. Kate cleaned her boots and then went an errand for her mother before going to the park. Mary was nowhere to be seen so Kate played with some other children and at about three in the afternoon she went home. Esther Jordan and Jane Cooper, who was Mary's older sister, were also in the park from about eleven in the morning to two in the afternoon, but saw no sign of her.

When Mary did not come home for tea, her mother became alarmed and the officer in charge of the Grange Road Police Station, PC Baghall, was informed who immediately sent out a description of the missing girl. The last sighting of her was on the east side of the park beside the lake at the spot where boats were hired out. On Sunday the police dragged the lake while Mary's mother and other family members went to Stockton to search for her. Mary's father, William, was an engineer on the steamer *Gwendoline*, which had sailed from St Malo for Middlesbrough on the previous Monday, so was at the moment, still at sea.

Bell's Hill, Albert Park where Mary's body was found. Norman Moorsom

On Monday afternoon, three young boys, William Cousins, Herbert Cousins and Edward Whitfield, were playing cricket on the northeast side of the park near Bell's Hill. The area was thus named because of the bell that was rung to clear the park prior to locking the gates at sunset. The ball went into a shrubby area that divided the cricket ground from a winding path. Herbert went to retrieve the ball when he saw a hat. He returned to his pals and told them that there was a lady's hat in the bushes. William went to look and saw what he thought was a child asleep. Her hat was on her face, her pinafore and dress were pulled up to her mouth and her petticoat was down. He called the other boys and one of them lifted the girl's arm, when it flopped back down they realised she was dead.

Mary Cooper on the left with her sister. Norman Moorsom

Horror stricken they ran to a woman that was standing nearby, she in turn went to the park gardener for help, he blew his whistle and PC Morrison, who was still searching the park, came to the summons. The little girl was lying in long grass, in a small copse full of shrubbery and young trees. She was lying on her back with her legs spread out, her teeth clenched and her hands in tight fists clutching small handfuls of the long grass. The upper parts of her clothing and her hair were saturated with blood that had come from a deep gash that extended right across her throat. The PC lifted Mary's lifeless body and carried it to the parent's house. Mary's mother was still out searching for her little girl, so did not yet know what had taken place.

A little later that evening Dr Duncan McCuaig assisted by Dr Thomas Nixon performed a post-mortem. There was no sign of violence on her lower body so rape was ruled out. Death had been due to a three-inch gash to the throat, inflicted with what was probably a rather blunt pocketknife that had severed the jugular vein and the windpipe. The following day a boy handed a pocketknife into the police that he had found about twenty yards (18.3m) from where the murder had taken place. There were traces of rust and what could have been blood found on the knife, but it was not certain whether it was the murder weapon.

The Park Committee of the Middlesbrough Corporation held a meeting on Tuesday 24 June and it was decided that although the park was watched by a curator, six gardeners and the police, several members expressed concern that this was not enough, so it was resolved to ask the Watch Committee to appoint extra policemen to patrol. The members also put up a £100 reward for information leading to the arrest of the murderer. Bills to this effect were posted throughout Middlesbrough and the rest of the country.

Dr Duncan McCuaig who performed the post- mortem on Mary Cooper's body.
Author's Collection

The place where the child was found was within yards of a well-frequented area of the park and must have been within earshot of dozens of people, but no one heard anything. No reason for the crime was ever forthcoming and no suspects accused. It was commonly believed that Mary had been dragged to the spot by a perpetrator intending rape and perhaps he had been disturbed by a passer by, so killed the little girl before she could raise the alarm. At a later inquest the father was questioned as to whether he had any enemies that would do something like this for spite. His answer was that he did not know of anyone who would do such a thing. The jury returned a verdict of murder by person or persons unknown.

William Cooper was not told of his daughter's death until his ship docked in Middlesbrough in the early hours of the morning of Thursday 26 June. Mary Cooper's funeral service was held later that same day by the vicar of the Newport Road Presbyterian Church. Thousands of mourners lined the streets as her small coffin was taken to the new cemetery at Linthorpe to be interred.

The inscription on Mary's gravestone is only just decipherable today and reads:

The gravestone of Mary Cooper in Linthorpe Cemetery. Olive Perrin

WE HAD A LITTLE DAUGHTER ONCE
AND BRIGHT BLUE EYES HAD SHE
A VERY MILD AND WINNING CHILD
AND DEAR TO US WAS SHE
ONLY TO US A SHORT TIME LENT
WAS OUR SWEET MARY DEAR
GOD SOON RECLAIMED THE GIFT HE LENT
AND LEFT US WEEPING HERE.

Chapter 27

A Violent Robbery at Stranton 1886

One Friday night in May after a hard day's work as a caulker, James Farnham went for a quiet drink to the *Mill House* beerhouse in Throston Street, Stranton. There were a few other men in the bar but he did not strike up a conversation with anyone. Farnham paid for his drink with a half sovereign and as he put his change in his pocket, noticed that one of the men was watching him though he did not think anything of it at the time. As Farnham left at about eight in the evening to head for his home in Slake Terrace, Middleton, the man who had been watching at the bar followed him and said 'that he wanted many a pound in Middleton,' Farnham replied that he did not want any money from him. The man then shoved Farnham and knocked him down while swearing at him and threatening to 'cut his head off.' A female servant came out from the *Mill House* and persuaded the man to come back into the bar and she suggested that Farnham go home before there was more trouble. Accordingly, Farnham set off towards the gas works down a narrow road that crossed the rubbish tips. He had walked about 400 yards when another man that had been in the beerhouse came up behind him, spun him around and hit him on the mouth with something hard, knocking Farnham to the ground. He was then grabbed and held down by the first man while the second man went through his pockets and took the 11s 6d (58p) that he had in change. As they walked away Farnham shouted to them that 'he knew them and that if he lived until tomorrow they would hear more of this,' one of the men replying 'you don't know me.' Soon afterwards two passers by, seeing Farnham lying on the ground helped him up and assisted him to make his way home.

The following morning Farnham went to the police where a

doctor examined him. He had lost four teeth from his upper jaw, two were loose on his lower jaw, his gums were badly swollen and his bottom lip was cut nearly through in two places. Inspector Bowman of the West Hartlepool police went to the *Mill House* and spoke to the servant there, on her direction he arrested a Thomas Robinson and then went to Darlington Terrace where he spoke to Alexander Butcher about the assault. Butcher began uttering curses and became violent so the police had to take him to the cells by force. Later that afternoon both Robinson and Butcher were charged with robbery and violence on James Farnham.

An inquest was held at the West Hartlepool Police Court. Mrs Isabella Jamieson, landlady of the *Mill House*, told how Butcher had asked her to let him have a pint of beer and pay

The smaller of the buildings was West Hartlepool Police Station where the inquest was held on the robbery of James Farnham. Cleveland County Council, Libraries and Leisurre Department

the following day, as he had no money, but she had refused to serve him. Shortly afterwards Farnham had left and she saw Butcher and Robinson follow him, her servant then told her that there had been trouble outside. Nearly an hour later Robinson returned and after speaking to a man named Royle, they left together. Butcher returned just after that and she noticed that he had changed his trousers. He told her he had money now and stood a round for his friend and wife, bought himself three or four quarts of beer and proceeded to get drunk. Mrs Jamieson's servant also gave evidence to what she had seen and heard in the original confrontation. The bench committed the two men for trial at the Durham Assizes.

The jury found both men guilty and Robinson was sentenced to nine calendar months in gaol with hard labour, Butcher was sentenced to twelve calendar months and twenty-five strokes of the cat's tail.

Chapter 28

The Woman in the Flue
1888

In the nineteenth century the iron and steel industry was booming and in the closing years, the Seaton Carew Ironworks, controlled by the Carlton Iron Company was established, and producing 100,000 tons of pig iron annually, was the largest exporter in the United Kingdom of basic iron. Situated at Longhill at the far northern end of the peaceful little village of Seaton Carew, it was a large complex housing three blast furnaces and ten regenerative hot blast firebrick stoves. To allow for the disposal of the ash and waste, flues were constructed to run underneath the blast furnaces.

Until the coming of the railway and the boom of the iron industry and shipbuilding, the village of Seaton Carew was mainly concerned with agriculture, fishing and catering for the many visitors that made the most of the beautiful beach in the summer season. During the busy months the women would be employed in laundry work, cooking and cleaning whilst the men would look after the horses and carriages. In the winter because there was no work in the inns or guesthouses,

The peaceful village of Seaton Carew, 1888. Pattison's Pictures, Bowes Museum

collecting cockles and mussels and sea coal were pursuits that were carried out to supplement an often meagre income.

It was a bleak, cold winter's day on Sunday, 22 January. At six thirty in the morning before the weak, wintry sunshine had made an appearance, an engine cleaner by the name of William Bradley, who had been on duty since three o'clock that morning at the Seaton Carew Iron Works, was approached by a young fireman named Lawson who told him he thought he had seen a light in a dust flue that ran under the boilers, and on checking he had found a young woman lying there. Bradley followed Lawson with trepidation as to what would greet them because he knew the temperature in the flue to be about 140 degrees Fahrenheit. The woman was crouched up and unconscious, about a yard from where she lay was a torch lamp that was not lit. Between them, the men lifted the woman out and carried her to the weigh cabin and then sent for the village policeman, PC Atkinson. When he arrived he realised the woman, although still alive, was in a critical condition, so the local doctor was immediately summoned. Dr Biggart, after examining the woman, said that he thought, besides the gases she would have inhaled while in the flue, might have narcotic poisoning, probably laudanum, whether self administered or by someone else, he could not tell. (Laudanum, a sedative extracted from opium, was commonly used for sleeplessness, pain of every sort and nervous complaints). The good doctor spent about an hour and a half trying to revive the woman but although her breathing improved slightly she did not awaken, eventually he had her taken to the hospital. She never regained consciousness and died about three o'clock on the Monday morning.

Collecting sea coal at Seaton Carew, 1888. Pattison's Pictures, Bowes Museum

An inquest was begun on the Monday afternoon at the Borough Hall in Hartlepool. The coroner, Mr Settle, thought the death suspicious and stated there would be an investigation but first the woman had to be identified. He adjourned the inquest to Wednesday afternoon after instructing Dr Biggart to carry out a post-mortem.

The young woman was identified as Catherine Flanity, a single woman of twenty-two years of age. On enquiry, some of the events prior to her death were revealed. She had lived in the area for about four months, the last one of those months was spent living with her cousin, Mary Battle, at 35 Back Frederick Street in Hartlepool. Catherine's sister, Mary Flanity, who worked at the Raby Hotel in Northallerton, had last seen her in the November of 1887 at a hireling fair which Catherine had attended to try and procure work, but, according to Mary, Catherine had 'wasted a situation.' She then went to stay with friends at Old Trimdon until she eventually managed to get a place with a Mr Pearson of Hartlepool, where she was employed until the Wednesday prior to her death.

The girls' mother had died some time previously and although they assumed their father was still alive, they were not sure as he had moved from his home in Old Trimdon in April of 1887 to live in Bishop Auckland and they had not heard of him since. Before leaving, he had placed his furniture in the care of a Mr Jopling. On Friday 20 January, Mary had received a letter from Catherine stating she would not be staying at Back Frederick Street for long so she needed an immediate reply to the correspondence. The letter asked that Mary go to Trimdon and see to their father's furniture, Mary had the impression that her sister was worried that the Joplings' might have considered the furniture theirs by now as it had been there so long. The letter gave no hint of Catherine being depressed.

At the second inquest, held on Wednesday 25 January, Catherine's cousin, Mary Battle, stated that Catherine had stayed in bed from the Thursday night to the Saturday morning saying she was not feeling well. Mary had missed a bottle of laudanum and on being asked about it, Catherine said she had taken it to use to ease the pain in her tooth. On Saturday night at about six o'clock, Catherine declared she was going to West

Hartlepool but did not say why or what she intended doing there.

The next sighting of Catherine was at the house of Jacob Barker and his father at Hill Street, Longhill. When a knock came at the door, Jacob opened it to a young woman who asked the time and directions to Hartlepool. Jacob told her it was about quarter to ten and he pointed out the way to Hartlepool. When she walked away from the door she went in the opposite direction to his instructions. He followed her but she turned a corner and disappeared from his sight. A little later Lawson (the young man who eventually found the woman in the flue) arrived at Jacob's house and stayed about a half hour, they then left together to go to Lawson's father's house. While they were there, Lawson's sister came in and said there was a man and a woman in the back street; when they went to look they saw a woman but no man. The mysterious woman walked up Florence Street and then down to the bottom of Hill Street, which was not in the direction of Hartlepool. Jacob said he heard her speak to two boys of about fifteen and eighteen years of age, saying 'I've got something which will cause me not to live to see morning.' Jacob, Lawson and the two boys she had spoken to then followed her across the field because they thought she looked 'queer.' Mary Jenkins, a single lady who lived in Florence Street, West Hartlepool was crossing the field on the path between the iron works and the glass works at about ten thirty on Saturday night when she passed the four boys without speaking to them, a little further on she came across a woman in a stooping position. Mary asked the woman if she was lost and she replied that she was but that she did not know where she wanted to go. The four boys then came up to Mary and told her they had spoken to the woman and she was lost, so Mary asked them to see the woman onto Mainsforth Terrace which Lawson said they would do. Mary later identified the body of Catherine as the woman on the field path and said that when she had spoken with her, Catherine seemed of sound mind and was definitely not drunk.

Jacob said that the four of them walked with the woman until they reached the blast furnace gate where the woman said 'that would do.' As they were leaving her she said to one of them 'Come my canny Irish lad, show me the way.' The boys then left her, walked to the bottom of Hill Street and separated. They were only a few yards from Lawson's house by then and Jacob stated that they never touched the woman and he went off to his own house and did not leave it again that night. The time by then was about eleven thirty.

PC Atkinson, giving his evidence at the inquest stated that the lamp found in the flue belonged to the Seaton Carew Iron Works Company and could have been left by one of the cleaners, although there had not been a cleaner on duty that night. He also said that for a stranger, with no knowledge of the lay out of the work's premises, to be able to find their way into the flue seemed most unlikely. A sketch of the area in which Catherine was found showed she would have had to have climbed a five foot wall and then clambered down a steep incline to reach the entrance to the flue and then travel about thirty yards (27.5m) along a channel that was about two and a half feet wide by four and a half feet high to reach the spot where she was found. This would not have been an easy feat, wearing the long, heavy skirts that were the apparel of the women of her class at that time.

Lawson had said he had seen a light in the flue and that was what had led him to discover the woman, but when he returned with Bradley the torch lamp was unlit and a small distance from where Catherine was lying, also it was assumed that when found, she had been unconscious for some time. William Bradley gave evidence that Lawson had told him that he had seen the woman enter the flue the previous night. Lawson said the same to the Coroner and regarding the torch lamp he said he had never seen it before and although it belonged to the company it should not have been there. Although Lawson was questioned, as he was only seventeen it was not deemed necessary to take his evidence. He denied saying that he had seen the woman enter the flue, only that he saw the woman go towards it, and that he and the other three boys had only shown her the way and had not touched her. He was not questioned further about the light he said had led him to the flue in the first place.

The post-mortem revealed no signs of violence. The lungs were very congested and showed evidence that she had once had pleurisy. Dr Biggart reported that when a piece of lung was

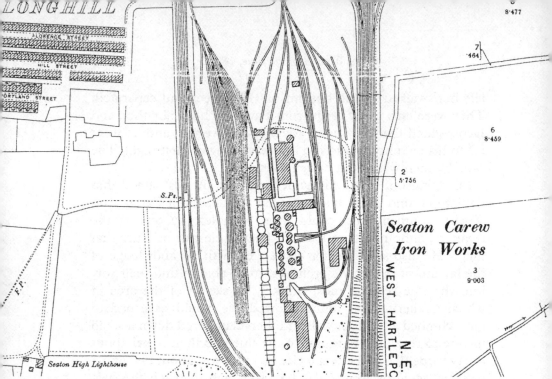

Location of the Seaton Carew Ironworks and the Longhill estate where Catherine Flanity spent her last hours. Ordnance Survey, Stranton 1896

cut off and placed in water it sank, showing that no air could pass through the lungs. He gave the cause of death as asphyxia due to the temperature and the length of time she may have been in the flue. Nothing more was mentioned regarding narcotic poisoning. The Coroner, on summing up, said it was a curious case as there was no evidence to show how she came to be in the flue. The jury returned a verdict of 'death by asphyxia.' Catherine was then buried in West Hartlepool cemetery.

Did Jacob really here the woman say 'I've got something which will cause me not to see morning.' The two boys that she was supposed to say this to were never identified so there was no one to dispute Jacob's statement. Lawson had stated that he had seen the woman enter the flue on the Saturday night and then he changed his story saying he had only seen her go towards the flue. Lawson also said a light had drawn him to investigate, but when Bradley went into the flue, there was no light. Mary Jenkins said that the woman had been fine when she spoke to her, but Jacob said she was acting 'queer.'

Was it just a terrible accident, a suicide, a boyish prank or did something more sinister result in the death of Catherine Flanity.

Chapter 29

Annie
1890

In the early hours of one Sunday morning a house in Stockton was the scene of a murder that was later described as one of the most terrible crimes that had ever been committed in the county.

The house was a lodging house at 1 Alberto Street, and was occupied by six people: Mrs Mary Jane McDonald (the landlady); Thomas Lockwood and another young man who had rooms upstairs, Mrs McDonald's eight year old daughter; Clare Mossom slept in the kitchen and lastly nineteen-year-old Sarah Ann Merryweather (better known as Annie), rented the front parlour, which was separated from the kitchen by an entrance passage. She had been lodging there for about eight weeks. Prior to moving into the lodging house, she had come from Northallerton to work as a servant on a farm at Thornaby, South Stockton for a justice of the peace, Mr Mark Robinson and she had then worked for Mr Blackburn of

A hirings fair in Stockton High Street. Cleveland County Council, Libraries and Leisure Department

A car park in Bishop Street, Stockton 2002, once the location of the Star Hotel.
The Author

Stockton. For a time Annie had kept company with Mr Blackburn's son, William, who had spoken to her last on the corner of Yarm Lane at the hirings fair on Wednesday 7 May.

Annie then started to keep company with Frederick Terry who was twenty-one and came from a well-respected family. His father had recently retired from the position of manager of the gas works at Croft near Darlington. Frederick had worked under his father until his retirement and had then moved to Stockton to work as a labourer for Messrs Blair and Co in their marine engineering shop. Annie and Frederick were often seen together in the street and in the *Star Hotel*, Bishop Street and other public bars in Stockton.

On Saturday evening 10 May, Clare Mossom and her friend Maude were in the *Star Hotel* when Frederick came in asking if they had seen Annie. They said they had not. Frederick bought both the girls a small claret and then left. At about eleven that night, Clare was on her way home when she saw Frederick standing in Norton Road. He said he was waiting for

Annie to come out of the pork shop then they were going back to the lodging house where he was going to spend the night with her. Clare waited with him and when Annie returned they all walked back to Mrs McDonald's together. They chatted for a little while and then went to their rooms.

The house was quiet until the early hours of the following morning when at about five o'clock, everyone was awoken by a woman's piercing scream. Thomas Lockwood was the first to react. On rushing downstairs and opening the parlour door a horrifying scene met his eyes. Annie, who was now silent, dressed only in a chemise and petticoat, was partly kneeling on the floor whilst Frederick had hold of her arm with his left hand and in his right hand was a razor. Thomas pushed Frederick aside, grabbed Annie and pulled her out through the door, locking it from the outside as he did so. Leaving her with the rest of the household, who were now all in the kitchen, he ran out of the house and down North Road towards the Central Buildings where Sergeant Morrison was on beat duty. The Sergeant accompanied Thomas back to Alberto Street and into the kitchen but by then Annie was dead. She had been repeatedly slashed with the razor. There were wounds to the insides of her fingers, probably inflicted as she tried to protect herself, deep gashes on her arms, breast, face and two others on her neck, one of which had caused her death by severing her jugular vein and causing her to bleed to death within a few minutes. The sergeant and Thomas unlocked the door to the parlour to find Frederick sitting quietly on the bed. The razor was lying on the iron framework at the top of the bed and the room looked like a slaughterhouse with blood spattered over the sparse furniture and all over the walls and floor. Frederick's clothes, hands and face were also covered in blood. Frederick admitted to the razor being his, but denied knowing Annie's name. The Sergeant told him to put his boots on and took him into custody.

At the inquest on the following Wednesday it came to light that the razor had been purchased from Mr Power's shop in the High Street on the Friday before the murder. Asked whether he had bought it with the intention of using it on Annie, Frederick replied that he did. The jury found him guilty of murder and he was committed for trial to Durham Assizes. Frederick showed no emotion or remorse throughout the proceedings.

At the trial, Frederick's defence pleaded insanity. He had been examined by Dr Smith of Sedgefield Asylum who found him 'of decidedly weak mental power, more like a boy of sixteen than a man of twenty-one.' Dr Shepherd also examined Frederick by order of the Home Office and his findings were that he had delusions and was of unsound mind. Another fact that came to light was that Frederick's brother was in Edinburgh Asylum. The prosecution said that the murder had been a particularly horrific, premeditated assault on a young defenceless girl. The razor had been purchased in advance with the sole intention of using it to maim or kill and because of this Frederick should be condemned to death.

The judge commented that nearly any man could trace a relative that suffered some mental derangement that did not mean that they themselves would succumb to insanity, also that Frederick Terry was quite sane at the present moment but if the jury felt that he was not responsible for his actions when he committed the murder then they must find him insane.

The jury retired and after an hour returned a verdict of 'guilty but of unsound mind.' The judge ordered that Frederick Terry be detained in an asylum during Her Majesty's Pleasure.

Chapter 30

Murder at John Street in Stockton 1891

In the month of August, the police were called to a narrow alleyway that led from Bishopton Lane to Albert Road in a poor locality in the centre of the town. There they entered a cheaply furnished but clean, two-storey house with a tiny yard, two rooms and a small scullery at 5 John Street. In the scullery was a coal closet that had a four-inch board at the front to keep the coal from falling out. Lying with her head over this board was the body of a woman. The woman's injuries were horrific, her head had been battered so severely that her right eye was completely destroyed and her throat was cut so deeply that her head had been almost severed from her body. Nearby was an axe covered with hair and stained with blood. On the table were two cups of cocoa, probably intended for breakfast. The police had the body removed to the mortuary.

The woman was Ann White and was aged forty-three. She had originally come from near Pickering and a letter that was found in the house, dated 23 June, from Thorton-le-Dale, was from her sister informing her of their mother's death from influenza. The police also found a note in a magazine written to Ann. It read,

Dear Ann,
Thank thee for the fish. I love thee with all my heart. May God bless thee. Forget me not. Let nothing part us but death.
From James Cook, your true lover.

About an hour after the police had left the scene a man walked into the police station saying he wanted to give himself up for the murder. The man's name was William Wood He was employed as a blacksmith at the Malleable Ironworks in Stockton and had been living with Ann for quite a few years.

They had two boys, one aged ten and the other eleven. It was one of the boys who, on coming downstairs in the morning, had discovered his mother's body.

A post-mortem revealed that, although the cause of death was the terrible wound to her throat that had severed her windpipe, arteries and cut through to her vertebrae, she would not have survived the head injuries.

William Wood, or 'Snowball' as his friends knew him, said it was jealousy that made him kill her. While she was kneeling, cleaning the fender, he had come up behind her and beaten her about the head with a chopping axe, then cut her throat with a knife 'to put her out of her misery.' He said that he had then gone to some water on the Norton Road, intending to drown himself, but instead had given himself up to the police.

The note the police had found in the magazine was from James Cook, the cause of Wood's jealousy. Cook lived in Cooper Street and according to Wood visited his house nearly every day, also that Cook had slept with Ann at the house, presumably while Wood was at work. He told the police to ask one of his sons, because he knew it to be true but the son was not questioned. None of the neighbours had ever seen Cook at Wood's house. Cook later admitted to writing the note and giving it to one of Ann's sons to deliver to her. Previous to the murder, Ann and James Cook had spent the day at Scarborough and had their photo taken together. Ann, on her return, told Wood that Cook was going to bring the photo and show him. The following morning, Ann had risen about seven thirty and gone about her usual business of cleaning the house but by nine o'clock she was dead.

A huge crowd turned up at the inquest, but they could not all fit into the courtroom and many of them had to remain outside. The note from Cook and the photo of Ann and Cook that was taken at Scarborough were produced and shown to the jury. Cook attended the trial, and, glowering at the prisoner, cuddled Wood's two sons, even giving each of them a ball. It transpired that Cook was a widower and Ann was his late wife's cousin who used to clean for him. Enquiries into Wood and his family had found that Wood's sister was an inmate of the imbecile ward at the Barnsley workhouse. A Dr

Pearson from South Stockton was called to give evidence. He had previously been an assistant superintendent at Colney Hutch Asylum, so was considered experienced enough to state an opinion. On examining the prisoner, he said that he found him to be a man slightly deaf, of feeble intelligence and showing symptoms of the early stage of general paralysis of the insane. Three other medical experts were called upon for an opinion and all agreed that Wood was bordering on insanity.

William Wood was found guilty of murder and committed to trial at the Durham Assizes. His plea of insanity was also ignored at the assizes and he was found guilty of murder and sentenced to death with a plea for mercy. A reprieve was granted and he was sentenced to life in penal servitude.

Ann was buried at Oxbridge Lane with none of her family in attendance, but the streets were lined with people as the cortege wound its way to the cemetery.

A neighbour took in Ann's children until a suitable institution could be found to house them. Number 5 John Street was locked and empty but remained an object of curiosity to crowds of people visiting the house for weeks after the event.

Oxbridge Lane Cemetery, Stockton, where Ann Wood was buried. The Author

Chapter 31

A Linthorpe Policeman
1893

On the north side of the suburban village of Linthorpe was an area known as Brick's Field. In a caravan on the field lived an elderly man of eighty-four, Henry Gould, and his family. They had originally come to the area fifty years previous with Wombwell's Menagerie and had lived in caravans ever since. Henry was a slaughter man and his son, John Henry, assisted Gould in his work. Henry, for some weeks, had been expressing concern about his son. He had told friends and neighbours that he was worried about the way John had been handling a muzzle-loading gun. John had threatened someone to whom he held a grudge and had pointed the gun at them.

Eventually Henry became so worried that he took possession of the gun, a revolver and a pistol and hid them. He then went to see a doctor, and after explaining his concerns, Dr Scanlan agreed to visit John and did so on 14 April. The doctor did not let on the reason for his visit. Instead he used diplomacy and told John that he had come to ask him to shoot a horse. John started talking nonsensically, saying that he was a piece of machinery and had been torn to bits by the machinery. He ended up by telling the doctor to shoot the horse himself. Dr Scanlan left the caravan and after writing up his report spoke to the relieving officer of Linthorpe at the police station, Mr Scotson and the sanitary inspector, Mr Anderson. The doctor told them that in his opinion John Gould was a lunatic. The three then headed for the caravan. As they approached, Henry Gould ran out to the road, his arm was covered in bruises and blood. Henry told the three men that he his son was waiting with a loaded gun and the bruises were the result of trying to take the gun from him.

On the advice of the doctor, the three men returned to

Linthorpe and spoke to Sergeant Black and PC Henderson. The doctor then left to attend to his duties. The other four men returned to the caravan to arrest John. As they approached they saw John in the yard holding the gun, beside him was a large mastiff dog. John shouted that he would shoot the first one that came near. Henry Gould enticed the dog away and tied it up. Meanwhile the four men separated and began creeping towards the gunman. When PC Henderson was just a few feet away he lunged forward to grab the gun but as he did so John fired. The policeman was killed instantly. The other three managed to restrain John and he was taken into custody.

PC Henderson was only thirty-eight and left behind a wife and eight children, the youngest a two month old set of twins. Originally he had come from West Auckland and had been in the police force for ten years. Although Mrs Henderson would receive money from the police superannuation fund it would not be sufficient to keep her and her children so a fund for public subscription was started. PC Henderson was buried in the New Linthorpe Cemetery.

John Gould was sent to Northallerton Gaol to await his trial at Leeds Assizes. The jury found him not responsible for his actions so therefore insane. He was ordered to be detained in a lunatic asylum at Her Majesty's Pleasure.

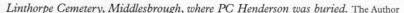

Linthorpe Cemetery, Middlesbrough, where PC Henderson was buried. The Author

Chapter 32

Rough Justice
1894

In the month of July, the town of Stockton was rocked by the brutal murder of a thirty-nine year old woman at 28 Henzell Street. The victim was Margaret Lawson, her husband, John, the perpetrator.

The couple had five children aged from three to sixteen and an older widowed daughter, Elizabeth Sharp, whose house they all lived in. John was a labourer and was often away for weeks at a time. He would tell the family that he was looking for work but never sent money home and they never knew where he was. When John was at home he would sometimes stay in bed all day. The mother and the two eldest daughters did washing and cleaning to support the family.

Margaret Jane, who was sixteen, had witnessed the attack and related what took place. Her father had been at home for about a month and had gone out on the Wednesday morning and returned at seven o'clock. He had not been drinking but

High Street, Stockton in 2002. The Author

angry words were exchanged because their mother and Elizabeth did not want him staying at the house any longer. He had been sleeping in a room upstairs while her mother and the children slept downstairs. Margaret Jane, Elizabeth and their mother slept in the same bed and had retired about eleven thirty on Wednesday night. At four in the morning Margaret Jane was awoken by her father coming into the room, he did not speak but put out the lamp that was burning. At this her mother awoke and asked what he wanted, when John answered 'nothing,' she told him to go, as they wanted a little more sleep. Her father then walked around to the other side of the bed and took hold of Elizabeth by the hair and struck her on the head. Their mother jumped out of bed to protect Elizabeth and John struck his wife. Margaret Jane saw the handle of a knife in his hand. Her mother had been stabbed just above the heart and when Margaret Jane realised he was going to stab their mother again, dragging the injured Elizabeth with her, she ran into the street screaming for help.

When she returned with her aunt, who lived a few doors away, and a policeman, her mother was lying on the floor bleeding profusely. Beside her was John, who was also bleeding from a cut on his throat. A large gully (kitchen) knife was on the floor beside him.

Elizabeth and John were seriously injured and were taken to the surgical hospital. Margaret Lawson was dead, having been stabbed sixteen times, mainly in the neck and breast. An inquest was held into her murder and John Lawson was found guilty but could not go to trial because of his injuries. He had stabbed himself in the throat twice and could not speak or swallow, as the injury had penetrated through the larynx into the pharynx. He was being fed through a nasal tube.

John Lawson never made it to his trial as he died of his injuries the following Thursday. An inquest took place and a verdict of *felo-de-se* (suicide) was returned. The judge decreed that under the circumstances the body could not have a Christian burial so preparations would have to be made for the interment. It was also pointed out that at one time the body would have been taken to four cross roads and a stake driven through it. That barbarous system had been terminated in the

Stockton Surgical Hospital where Elizabeth Sharp and John Lawson were taken. The Author

reign of George IV, and so prevented the forfeiture of the goods and chattels of the deceased.

Margaret Lawson was buried at Oxbridge cemetery. The procession consisted of five coaches and many mourners following on foot. Thousands of spectators lined the streets because the funeral took place at the time of the hospital demonstrations. John Lawson was also buried at Oxbridge, but was taken at midnight by the shortest route and was interred with no mourners and no Christian prayers.

The four younger children were placed in a Bristol orphanage. The jurors had been paid 1s (5p) for their services, and every one gave the shilling to sixteen-year-old Margaret Jane.

Oxbridge lane Cemetery, where Margaret and John Lawson were buried. The Author

Chapter 33

Murder at Newport
1894

Davd Bell was fifty-five and worked as a fitter for Messrs Samuelson & Co for thirty years. He had been married but had left his wife some years before and she had since died. Bell was living with Annie Burnett, who was fifty and had seven children. They resided with two of the children at number 7 Old Buildings, Newport, which, it was said, had once been a monastery.

Bell had a drink problem, but on this particular night he was quite sober. He had gone looking for PC Davey at his house in Ayresome Road but he was not at home. Eventually Bell found the constable in Newport Road and told him that he had had words with his housekeeper, then killed her. PC Davey

Map showing the location of the Cannon Street Police Station where David Bell was taken after admitting to murdering his partner. Ordnance Survey, Middlesbrough 1913.

escorted Bell to Cannon Street police station and from there he was taken by tramcar to the central police office where he was formally charged. No weapon was found on Bell's person but his hands were covered in blood.

The body of Annie Burnett was lying on a mat in the room occupied by the couple and three neighbours were preparing to lay her out. The neighbours told the police that Annie had been sitting by the fire sewing when her little daughter, who had been upstairs, heard her cry out. When her daughter came into the room, Annie was dying of a stab wound to her throat.

The room was spacious with cheap lithographs adorning the walls. It was scrupulously clean except for a large pool of blood that was still trickling over the tiled floor.

Bell was charged with 'murder with malice aforethought' and sent to Northallerton for the inquest. He admitted to the murder but denied 'malice aforethought' saying he had committed the deed 'in a fit of passion.' His story was that he had been paring the corns on his feet with a penknife when a quarrel had started. Annie had grabbed the knife and in the ensuing struggle her throat had been cut. Medical evidence was to the contrary as the knife had been used more than once. The neighbours who lived in the rooms in the same building had heard no noise or arguing.

The neighbours had known Bell for many years and all agreed that he, although of late had been drinking a lot, was a mild, inoffensive man. The couple had only been living together for nine months. Annie had been a charwoman and was a hard worker and well thought of locally.

Nelly Burnett, Annie's nine-year-old daughter stated that the couple had been sitting by the fire talking about getting married. Annie had said she did not want to get married and Bell had called her 'a f...... Irish pig' then Nelly had heard a cry and on going downstairs found her mother dying.

Bell was committed to York Assizes on the charge of murder with a strong recommendation of mercy. The verdict was the same as it had been at the inquest and Bell was sentenced to death. At the last minute he received a reprieve and was instead sentenced to life in penal servitude.

Chapter 34

Neglect, Dirt and Drink
1894-98

Throughout the nineteenth century, cases of child neglect all seemed to have an underlying similarity. Both in the way the children were neglected and in the reasons for the neglect.

1894: The Horans

There were three children in the Horan family, aged one, three and six years. The oldest boy had been found wandering in Stockton with no shoes on, hardly any clothes and covered in vermin. He was also bleeding from several wounds on his body. The police visited the house of his parents, Julia and Thomas Horan. They found the house to be extremely filthy and there was only one bed. The youngest child was less than half the body weight it should have been and was terribly emaciated.

When questioned Julia said that she could not see what the fuss was about. Thomas told the police that his wife would not clean up or look after the children and he had despaired of her. He was out of work and had been on parish relief for more than a month.

The court decided that Thomas was to be pitied rather than blamed but Julia was sentenced to two months in prison. The court ordered that the children be removed from their parent's home and taken to the Middlesbrough shelter until a permanent institution could be found for them.

1894: The Smiths

William Smith and his wife lived in Cannon Street, Middlesbrough. They had a daughter, Jane, who was three and a half years old. William had taken out insurance on Jane's life.

The parents went out for a drink one evening, leaving Jane

Middlesbrough Town Hall, built in 1889.
Author's Collection

and another child of about the same age, who was in their care, alone in the house. An unguarded coal fire was burning away merrily in the grate, so of course, the inevitable happened and Jane was so severely burnt that she died.

The verdict by a jury was accidental death, with a request to the coroner to reprimand the parents. The coroner stated that it was suspicious that the child's life had been insured at so tender an age, and the parents were guilty of little short of murder. He was referring the case to the Society for the Prevention of Cruelty to Children and hoped they would take the matter further. Also the coroner said that he would do everything in his power to prevent the insurance payment being made.

1898: The Mahoneys

Mary Ann Mahoney's husband had a good job at the Middlesbrough shipyards. He earned 30s (£1.50) a week plus overtime and handed nearly all of it to his wife. Sadly, Mary Ann spent the money on drink and not on her home or children. Nearly all the children's clothes had been pawned to buy drink as well. The children were all underweight, were

Middlesbrough shipyards in the nineteenth century. Pattison's Pictures, Bowes Museum.

covered in lice as big as fleas and the house was filthy.

Mary Ann had been convicted of neglect in the past and had served six months in prison. While she was locked up, her husband and the eldest daughter cleaned up the house and began to right things a little. When Mary Ann was released things became as bad as ever.

Mary Ann was returned to prison, this time for three months.

1898: The Midgleys

Charles Midgley was a shoemaker and in addition he had worked as a lamplighter for the West Hartlepool Corporation. He was dismissed from the corporation for drunkenness. Charles was a widower with seven children, four of whom still lived with him.

His late wife's relatives helped out with the children as much as possible, but Charles spent most of his money on drink. He was reported to the police and they duly inspected the house. They found that the children were half starved, had hardly any clothing and were covered in vermin. It also transpired that Charles would boil peas and potatoes, he would then eat the vegetables and give the children the water they were cooked in telling them it was soup.

Charles was found guilty of shameful neglect and sentenced to four months hard labour.

West Hartlepool Town Hall in 2002. The Author

Chapter 35

A Jealous Frenzy
1899

One night in May, a house in Ada Street, which ran at right angles to Hart Road in West Hartlepool, was the scene of a terrible tragedy. A coloured man, Thomas Thompson shot his wife and then cut the throat of their lodger, Isaac Phillips.

Emily Thompson had just gone to bed when suddenly her husband fired a revolver. The first bullet caught her on the left side of the chest and the second penetrated her neck. Phillips heard the shots, burst into the bedroom and after a struggle, managed to get take the revolver from Thompson and run downstairs. The next-door neighbour, Liddle, had also heard the shots and on running towards the house, met Phillips at the front door, who handed him the revolver and told him to go for the police. Phillips then went back into the house, presumably to check on Emily's condition.

When Liddle returned with PC Taylor, Phillips and Thompson were on the floor in a life and death struggle. Phillips had a large gash to his throat that had been inflicted with a penknife and Thompson had his hands in the wound as if he was trying to tear it open. PC Taylor managed to pull Thompson off Phillips and restrain him with handcuffs. Meanwhile, Emily had managed to drag herself downstairs and into Liddle's house where she collapsed in the lobby. Liddle went for medical assistance. Dr Hawley and Dr MacGregor attended and pronounced that there was nothing they could do for Emily as she had lost too much blood. Both the injured were removed to hospital where Dr MacGregor stitched the deep wound on Phillips' throat. Thompson was told his wife was in a critical condition and he said:

Oh officer, let me kiss her before she dies. I don't care now what becomes of me. I can do her no more harm than I have done already. I am sorry for what I have done. She has brought the trouble on both herself and me.

Emily died early the following morning and Thompson was charged with her murder.

It appeared that Emily had a child, who was now ten, to another man and although her husband seemed to forgive her, he had not forgotten. They had taken Phillips in as a lodger a few months before the tragedy and Thompson had become jealous of him. This had given rise to frequent quarrels and only recently, Emily had taken out a summons against her husband for assault. The hearing was to have been the following week. PC Taylor stated that Emily had complained to him of her husband's violence and on one occasion he had seen her with two black eyes.

Thompson's version of the event was that his wife was too friendly with the lodger and he had told Phillips on numerous occasions to leave, but he would not go. That fateful night he said that his wife was downstairs with Phillips and although he shouted to her twice, she would not come to bed. Thompson also said that he had warned them of what he would do to them. He then said that the gun had gone off accidentally and that he did not know that Emily had been shot. The penknife had fallen from his pocket and he had picked it up and cut Phillips without thinking.

Six days later Phillips died from complications arising from the injury he had received, so Thompson was now charged with two murders. He was committed to the Durham Assizes for trial.

Justice Grantham thought that Thompson's story was highly improbable. The jury brought in a verdict of 'guilty of murder with a strong recommendation for mercy on the grounds of provocation.' He was sentenced to death.

On 18 August the death sentence was revoked and he was instead committed to life in prison. Thompson was transferred to Stafford Gaol to serve his term.

Sources

1. Longstaffe, *History and Antiquities of Darlington*, pp 310-311, 320-321.
2. *Haydn's Dictionary of Dates*, London 1895.
3. B J D Harrison and G Dickson (Editors), *Guisborough Before 1900*.
4. *Hartlepool Free Press*, 1855-72.
5. *South Durham Herald*, 1866-91.
6. *Stockton and Hartlepool Mercury* and *Middlesbrough News*, 1855-65.
7. *South Durham and Cleveland Mercury*, 1867-1900.
8. *Stockton and Hartlepool Mercury* and *Middlesbrough News*, 4 August 1855.
9. *South Durham Herald*, 22 July 1871.
10. *South Durham Herald* and *Stockton Journal*, 23 May 1885.
11. *Stockton and Hartlepool Mercury*, 9 March 1861.
12. *Hartlepool Free Press*, 2 April 1864.
13. *South Durham Herald* and *Cleveland Mercury*, 28 May 1870.
14. *South Durham Herald* and *Cleveland Mercury*, 3 March 1873.
15. *South Durham Herald* and *Stockton Journal*, 29 August 1891.
16. *South Durham Herald*, 21 July 1899.
17. Robert Woodhouse, *Stockton-on-Tees: A Pictorial History.*

Acknowledgements

I would like to thank all the following for their invaluable assistance with illustrations:
The Art Archive, London; Durham Arts, Libraries and Museums; Bowes Museum, Barnard Castle;
Cleveland County Council, Libraries and Leisure Department; Brian Elliott; Norman Moorsom;
John and Olive Perrin and Geoff and Jenny Braddy.

Index